Discovering the LIGHTHOUSES *of North America*

Discovering the
LIGHTHOUSES
of North America

ANNELISE HOBBS

ERMINE
STREET

BOOKS

PUBLISHED IN 2011 BY
ERMINE STREET BOOKS
AN IMPRINT OF
REGENCY HOUSE PUBLISHING LTD.

**COPYRIGHT © 2011 REGENCY
HOUSE PUBLISHING LIMITED**
UNIT P1, WATERMILL INDUSTRIAL ESTATE
ASPENDEN ROAD
BUNTINGFORD
HERTFORDSHIRE
SG9 9JS
UNITED KINGDOM

ISBN-13: 978-1-85361-601-3

PRINTED IN CHINA

Contents

CHAPTER ONE
A HISTORY OF THE LIGHTHOUSE

A lighthouse is a tower, building or other structure designed to emit light from a system of lamps and lenses or, in older times, from fires, and used as an aid to navigation for pilots at sea or on inland waterways.

Lighthouses are used to mark dangerous coastlines, hazardous shoals and reefs, also safe entries to harbours, and can also assist in aerial navigation. Once widely used, the number of operational lighthouses has declined due to the expense of their maintenance and their replacement by modern electronic navigational aids.

In a lighthouse, the source of light is called the 'lamp' (whether electric or fuelled

by oil) and the concentration of the light is achieved by the 'lens' or 'optic'.

Originally lit by open fires and later by candles, the Argand hollow-wick lamp and parabolic reflector was developed in around 1781 in Europe. Meanwhile, in the United States, whale oil was used with solid wicks as the source of light, until the Argand parabolic reflector system was introduced in around

1810 by Winslow Lewis. Colza oil replaced whale oil in the early 1850s, but a lack of interest in growing this commodity in the US necessitated the lighthouse service's switch to lard oil in the mid-1850s.

Kerosene began to replace lard oil in the 1870s and the service was finally totally converted by the late 1880s. Electricity and carbide (acetylene gas) gradually replaced

The Portland Head Light is an historic lighthouse located on Cape Elizabeth, Maine, the beacon and fog signal of which are owned and maintained by the US Coast Guard as a current aid to navigation.

kerosene at around the turn of the 20th century, the use of the latter promoted by the Dalén light (see page 19), which

automatically lit the lamp at nightfall and extinguished it at dawn.

LIGHTHOUSES OF THE ANCIENT WORLD

The use of lights as navigational aids goes back as far as the 8th century BC, for references to beacons built on hilltops to guide ships at sea occur in Homer's *Iliad* and *Odyssey* and the earliest works of European literature.

Perhaps the most famous lighthouse in history is the Pharos of Alexandria, built on

the island of Pharos in Hellenistic Egypt. The Greek word *pharos* is still used to describe a 'lighthouse' in some languages and the term 'pharology', or the study of lighthouses, also derives from the same root.

The Pharos of Alexandria was built in 280BC, and with a height estimated at 350ft was the tallest man-made structure of the

LEFT: The Pharos of Alexandria, a computer-generated illustration based on ancient records discovered by Hermann Thiersch in 1909.

ABOVE: The Liuhe Pagoda-Lighthouse is located on Yuelun Hill overlooking the Qiantang river.

OPPOSITE: The ruins of one of the lighthouses built by the Romans at Dover to protect the English Channel off the southern English coast.

ancient world after the pyramids of Giza; it was described as one of the Seven Wonders of the World by classical writers. Two other lighthouses, each known as *fara* in their time, and modelled on the *farum* built for Caligula's aborted invasion of Boulogne, were built on Dover's Eastern and Western Heights, in the south of England, soon after the Roman conquest of Britain in AD43.

The Colossus of Rhodes, situated on an island in the Aegean Sea, and another of the Ancient Wonders of the World, is also believed to have been a lighthouse, and took the form of a 105-ft bronze statue of the god Helios, standing astride the entrance to Mandrákion harbour.

In his work written between 785 and 805, Jia Dan described the sea route through the mouth of the Persian Gulf, and that the medieval Iranians (whom he called the people of Luo-He-Yi) had erected 'ornamental pillars' in the sea that acted as lighthouse beacons for ships that might go astray. This was confirmed a century later by Arab writers such as al-Mas'udi and al-Muqaddasi.

In China, the medieval mosque at Canton had a minaret that served as a lighthouse,

while the later Song Dynasty Chinese pagoda tower, built in medieval Hangzhou and known as the Liuhe Pagoda (erected in 1165), also served as a navigational aid along the Qiantang river.

During the Dark Ages, Roman lighthouses fell into disuse, but some remained functional, such as the Farum Brigantium, now known as the Tower of Hercules, at La Coruña, Spain, and others along the Mediterranean Sea.

As navigation improved, lighthouses gradually expanded into Western and Northern Europe, one of the oldest working lighthouses in Europe being the Hook Lighthouse, located on Hook Head in County Wexford, Ireland, and built during the medieval period to a sturdy circular design. A century later, also in the late Middle Ages, a 40-ft tower was built by Edward the Black Prince at Cordouan, near to the mouth of the Gironde river in France, while 100 years later, in 1581, Henri III asked architect Louis de Foix to survey it and estimate the cost of its repair. But this proved too costly an enterprise and de Foix was contracted three years later to build a new lighthouse.

Building the lighthouse took 27 years, and was finally completed in 1611, the tiered Cordouan lighthouse being a symbol of French maritime power and prestige. The interior had sumptuous apartments, intended for the king, decorated with ornate pillars and

OPPOSITE: Dating from the 12th century, Hook Lighthouse on Hook Head, in County Wexford, Ireland, is the oldest functional lighthouse in Europe.

RIGHT: The Tower of Hercules, at La Coruña, in Galicia, Spain, has been delegated a UNESCO World Heritage Site.

murals. Its upper level was rebuilt in 1788, and the lighthouse has remained active since that time.

The tower later became the first to use the revolutionary Fresnel lens in the early 1820s and greatly impressed the British civil engineer, Robert Stevenson, himself a famous builder of lighthouses. As Britain became the dominant seapower in the world, lighthouses constructed by the Stevenson family for the Northern Lighthouse Board began to appear all over Scotland.

OPPOSITE ABOVE: The Tour de Cordouan is the oldest functioning lighthouse in France.

OPPOSITE BELOW: The Eddystone Lighthouse guards the treacherous Eddystone Rocks off the Devon coast in England.

BELOW: The St. Augustine Light, Florida.

LIGHTHOUSES OF THE CLASSICAL PERIOD

Lighthouse development accelerated in the 17th century with Britain's Trinity House constructing its first lighthouse in 1609, and a national lighthouse service was established in Denmark in 1650. Also in Britain, the first Eddystone Lighthouse was lit in 1698, though its third incarnation, designed by John Smeaton and finished in 1759, proved to be the most enduring.

St. Augustine was the site of the first 'lighthouse' established in Florida by the new territorial American government in 1824. This 'official' lighthouse was placed on the site of an earlier watchtower built by the Spanish as early as the late 16th century. The map of St. Augustine, depicting Sir Francis Drake's

LEFT: The Boston Light is located on Little Brewster Island in outer Boston Harbor, Massachusetts. The first lighthouse to be built on the site dates back to 1716, and was the first to be built in what is now the United States. The current lighthouse dates from 1783, and is the second oldest working lighthouse in the US (after Sandy Hook Light in New Jersey), and is the only one still to be actively staffed by the United States Coast Guard.

OPPOSITE: The Sandy Hook Light, located about 1.5 miles inland from the tip of Sandy Hook, New Jersey, is the oldest working lighthouse in the United States.

attack on the city, by Baptista Boazio, in 1589, shows an early wooden tower near to the Spanish structure, which was described as a 'beacon' in Drake's account.

The next lighthouse in North America was the Boston Light on Little Brewster Island (1716). The first keeper was George Worthylake who drowned, along with his wife and daughter, when returning to the island in 1718. The original tower was destroyed by the British during the evacuation of Boston and was eventually reconstructed in 1784. America's oldest working lighthouse, however, is the Sandy Hook Light, New Jersey, built in 1764, and which is still in operation.

By the end of the 19th century, the United States, with its long coastline, had more lighthouses than any other nation.

The US Bureau of Lighthouses was created in 1789 by the 9th Act of the first Congress which placed lighthouses under federal control. Over the years, lighthouses came under the jurisdiction of the Department of Revenue (disbanded in 1820), the Department of Treasury (until 1903), then the

Department of Commerce. The Lighthouse Board (of the US Lighthouse Establishment) held sway from 1852 to 1 July 1910, when Commerce created the Lighthouse Service. The United States Coast Guard subsequently took over responsibility on 7 July 1939.

After 1852 the US was divided into Lighthouse Districts. Originally eight, they eventually numbered 19, and each was run by a naval officer appointed by the Lighthouse Board as district inspector; he ran the district in tandem with an officer of the Army Corps of Engineers, who was in charge of engineering projects, although by 1910, civilians had begun to replace the military.

The first lighthouse in Canada was the Louisbourg Light, built by the French in Nova

LEFT: Sambro Island Light, Halifax, is the oldest surviving lighthouse in North America.

ABOVE: Nils Gustaf Dalén invented the automatic lamp systems which made keepers obsolete.

Scotia in 1734, and destroyed during the Siege of Louisbourg in 1758. The British built the Sambro Island Light at Halifax, Nova Scotia, in the same year, which has survived to the present day, making it the oldest surviving lighthouse in North America.

The network of lighthouses built by the colonies of British North America were united in 1867 by the Canadian government, which greatly expanded the Canadian lighthouse system through the Canadian Department of Marine, largely by means of economical wooden lighthouses staffed by families.

Lighthouses were extremely labour-intensive during the classic era of lighthouse operation, in that keepers were needed to trim the wicks, replenish fuel, wind clockworks and perform maintenance tasks, such as cleaning lenses and windows.

In 1907, Nils Gustaf Dalén invented the sun-valve, which caused beacons to light automatically at dusk and extinguish themselves at dawn, enabling lighthouses to function perfectly and unattended for periods of up to a year. In 1912 Dalén was awarded the Nobel Prize for Physics for his invention of 'automatic valves designed to be used in combination with gas accumulators in lighthouses'.

Dalén's inventions, electrification and automatic lamp changers began to make lighthouse keepers obsolete, even though they contined to be used for many years, partly because they could act as a rescue service if necessary. Improvements in maritime navigation and safety, such as GPS, however, has led to the phasing out of non-automated lighthouses, with the last keepers having been removed in the 1990s.

MODERN LIGHTHOUSES

Often seen in inaccessible locations, modern lighthouses are more functional and less

LEFT: Gorge Smeaton, the designer of the Eddystone Lighthouse.

BELOW LEFT: General George Mead designed and built many lighthouses along the eastern seaboard of the United States.

BELOW: Colonel Orlando M. Poe was responsible for a number of beautiful lighthouses on the Great Lakes.

picturesque. They generally use solar-charged batteries and have single stationary flashing lights sitting on steel skeleton towers.

The last manned lighthouse built in the US was the Charleston Light, constructed in 1962. Resembling an air traffic control tower, it has a modern triangular shape, aluminium-alloy skin, air conditioning, and an elevator.

LIGHTHOUSES BUILDERS

John Smeaton is noteworthy for having designed the third and most famous Eddystone Lighthouse, but some are well-

known for building multiple lighthouses. The Stevenson family (Robert, Alan, David, Thomas, David Alan and Charles) made lighthouse-building a three-generation profession in Scotland, while Irishman Alexander Mitchell invented and built a number of screwpile lighthouses despite being blind.

Lieutenant George Meade, of the US Corps of Engineers, built numerous lighthouses along the Atlantic and Gulf coasts before gaining wider fame as the winning general at the Battle of Gettysburg in 1863, while Colonel Orlando M. Poe, engineer to General William Tecumseh Sherman in the Siege of Atlanta, designed and built some of the most exotic lighthouses in the most difficult locations on the Great Lakes. Alexander Ballantyne built two of the most challenging wave-washed lighthouses on barren rocks in the Pacific Ocean, these being the Tillamook Rock Light off the Oregon coast and the St. George Reef Light off the coast of California.

Englishman James Douglass was knighted for his work on lighthouses, and French merchant navy officer, Marius Michel Pasha, built hundreds of lighthouses along the coasts of the Ottoman Empire in a period of 20 years following the Crimean War (1853–1856).

LENS TECHNOLOGY

Prior to modern strobe lights, lenses were used to concentrate the light from a

LEFT: The Tillamook Rock Light, designed by Alexander Ballantyne, is a deactivated lighthouse off the Oregon coast of the United States.

OPPOSITE: The development of the Fresnal lens in 1822 revolutionized lighthouses.

continuous source. Two tasks were involved:
• Vertical light rays of the lamp are redirected into a horizontal plane
• Horizontally, the light is focused into one or a few directions at a time, with the light beam sweeping around; as a result, in addition to

seeing the side of the light beam, the light can be seen directly from a further distance away.

THE FRESNEL LENS

This concentration of light is accomplished with a rotating lens assembly. In lighthouses

of the classical period, the light source was a kerosene lamp or, earlier, an Argand lamp using animal or vegetable oil, and the lenses were rotated by a weight-driven clockwork assembly wound by lighthouse keepers, sometimes as often as every two hours. The

lens assembly was sometimes floated in mercury to reduce friction.

In more modern lighthouses, electric lights and motor drives were used, generally powered by diesel-electric generators. These also supplied electricity for the use of the lighthouse keepers and their families.

Development of the Fresnel lens in 1822 revolutionized lighthouses in the 19th century, focusing 85 per cent of a lamp's light as opposed to the 20 per cent focused with the parabolic reflectors of the time. Its design enabled construction of lenses of large size and short focal length without the weight and volume of material in conventional lens designs. Although the Fresnel lens was invented in 1822, it was not implemented in the US until the 1850s due to the parsimonious administrator of the United States Lighthouse Establishment, Stephen Pleasonton. With the creation of the United States Lighthouse Board in 1852,

BELOW: Third-order Fresnel lens from the Bolivar Point lighthouse, near Galveston, Texas, used from 1907–33.

OPPOSITE: The historic Makapu'u Point Lighthouse uses a very powerful lens.

all US lighthouses had been given Fresnel lenses by 1860.

Fresnel lenses were ranked by order, with a first-order lens being the largest, most

powerful and expensive and a sixth-order lens being the smallest. The order is based on the focal length of the lens. A first-order lens has the longest focal length, with the sixth having the shortest. Coastal lighthouses generally use first-, second- or third-order lenses, while harbour lights and beacons use fourth-, fifth- or sixth-order lenses.

Some lighthouses, such as those at Cape Race, Newfoundland, and Makapu'u Point, Hawaii, used a more powerful hyperradiant Fresnel lens manufactured by the firm of Chance Brothers.

In recent times, many Fresnel lenses have been replaced by rotating aerodrome beacons which require less maintenance. In modern automated lighthouses, this system of rotating lenses is often replaced by a high-intensity light that emits brief omnidirectional flashes (concentrating the light in time rather than direction). These lights are similar to obstruction lights used to warn aircraft of tall structures. Recent innovations are Vega lights, and initial experiments have been made with LED panels.

In any of these designs, rather than seeing a continuous weak light, an observer sees a brighter light during short-time intervals. These instants of bright light are arranged to create a light characteristic or pattern that is specific to the particular lighthouse. For example, in the Scheveningen Lighthouse in the Netherlands, time intervals between flashes are alternately 2.5 and 7.5 seconds.

Some lights have sectors of a particular colour (usually formed by coloured panes in the lantern) to distinguish safe water areas from dangerous shoals. Modern lighthouses often have unique reflectors or Racon transponders so that the radar signature of the light is also unique.

BUILDING DESIGN

To be effective, the lamp must be high enough to be seen in time before the danger is reached by a mariner. The minimum height is calculated according to trigonometry by taking the square root of the height of a lighthouse in feet and multiplying it by 1.17 to give the distance to the horizon in nautical miles.

Where dangerous shoals are located far off a flat sandy beach, the prototypical tall masonry coastal lighthouse is constructed to assist the navigator making a landfall after an ocean crossing. Often these are cylindrical to reduce the effect of wind on a tall structure, such as the Cape May Light in New Jersey. Smaller versions of this design are often used as harbour lights to mark the entrance into a port, such as the New London Harbor Light.

Where a tall cliff exists, a smaller structure may be placed on top, such as at the Horton Point Light. Sometimes, such a location can be too high – as along the west coast of the United States. In these cases, lighthouses are placed below clifftops to ensure that they can still be seen at the

OPPOSITE: The lighthouse at Scheveningen, Netherlands, has a distinctive light pattern, the time intervals between flashes being alternately 2.5 and 7.5 seconds.

ABOVE: Cylindrical lighthouses, such as the Cape May, are better able to withstand strong winds.

RIGHT: Point Reyes was built below the clifftop so that it has more chance of being seen in fog.

framework, such as in the Thomas Point Shoal Light on Chesapeake Bay. As screwpiles can be disrupted by ice, in northern climates steel caisson lighthouses, such as the Orient Point Light on Long Island are used, while the Orient Long Beach Bar Light (Bug Light) is a blend of a screwpile light that was later converted to a caisson light because of the threat of ice damage.

In waters too deep for a conventional structure, a lightship might be used instead of a lighthouse, although most of these have

OPPOSITE: The Old Point Loma Light was replaced by another lighthouse because, having been built on a clifftop, it was often shrouded in fog. The new lighthouse was built lower down.

LEFT and BELOW: Examples of screwpile lighthouses: the Thomas Point Shoal Light (left) and the Seven Foot Knoll Light (below).

now been replaced by fixed light platforms (such as the Ambrose Light) similar to those used for offshore oil exploration.

surface during periods of fog, as at Point Reyes Lighthouse in California. Another victim of fog was the Point Loma Light (old) which was replaced with a lower lighthouse, the Point Loma Light (new).

As technology advanced, prefabricated skeletal iron or steel structures tended to be used for lighthouses constructed in the 20th century. These often have a narrow cylindrical core surrounded by an open lattice-work bracing, such as in the Finns Point Range Light, that was located just east of the Delaware river.

Sometimes a lighthouse needs to be constructed in the water itself, these invariably being masonry structures, built to withstand water impact, such as the Eddystone Lighthouse in Britain and the St. George Reef Light off California. In shallower bays, screwpile ironwork structures are inserted into the seabed and a low wooden structure is placed above the open

for cleaning the outside of the windows of the lantern room.

Lighthouses near to one another, that are similar in shape, are often painted in unique patterns, known as daymarks, so that they can be easily recognized during daylight hours, the black-and-white barber pole spiral of the Cape Hatteras Light being one such example. The Race Rocks Light, in western Canada, is painted in horizontal black-and-white bands so that it stands out clearly against the horizon.

RANGE LIGHTS

Aligning two fixed points on land provides a navigator with a line of position called a range in the USA and a transit in Britain. Ranges can be used to align a vessel precisely within a narrow channel such as that in a river. With landmarks of a range illuminated with a set of fixed lighthouses, night-time navigation is therefore made possible.

Such paired lighthouses are called range lights in the USA and leading lights in Britain. Two lights are used in this scheme: the one closer to the vessel is named the beacon or front range; the furthest away is called the rear range. The rear range light is almost always taller than the front.

When the vessel is on the correct course, the two lights line up above one another. But when the observer is out of position, the difference in alignment indicates the proper direction of travel to correct the problem.

While lighthouse buildings differ depending on their location and purpose, they tend to have common components.

A light station comprises the lighthouse tower and all outbuildings, such as the keeper's living quarters, fuel house, boathouse, and fog-signalling building. The lighthouse itself consists of a tower structure supporting the lantern room where the light operates.

The lantern room is the glassed-in housing, at the top of a lighthouse tower, containing the lamp and lens. Its glass storm panes are supported by metal Astragal bars running vertically or diagonally. At the top of the lantern room is a storm-proof ventilator, designed to remove the smoke from the lamps and the heat that builds up in the glass enclosure. A lightning rod and grounding system, connected to the metal cupola roof, provides a safe conduit in the event of lightning strikes.

Immediately beneath the lantern room is usually a watchroom or service room where fuel and other supplies were kept and where the keeper prepared the lanterns for the night and often stood watch. The clockworks (for rotating the lenses) were also located there. On a lighthouse tower, an open platform, called the gallery, is often located outside the watchroom (called the main gallery) or lantern room (lantern gallery). This was used mainly

ABOVE LEFT: The lantern room of the Head Harbour Light, in New Brunswick, Canada.

OPPOSITE: The Boston Light is situated on Little Brewster Island in Boston Harbor. It was the first to be built in what is now the USA.

AMERICAN LIGHTHOUSES

Many of the earliest lighthouses predate the birth of the nation, the first lighthouse in the US arriving in 1716 in Boston Harbor, which encouraged other North Atlantic cities to build lighthouses as well, their purpose being to foster the growing maritime economy of the colonies. The waters of the North Atlantic were a 'superhighway', where shipping was concerned, and lighthouses served as the signs, signals and direction indicators in areas of crowded open waters. The lighthouses were also essential in that the marshy coastlines from Delaware to North Carolina often made navigation difficult, while the New England coast was particularly treacherous due to its rocky shores.

Navigation aids of this kind were therefore essential to the growth and continued survival of the British colonies in America, and the development of the lighthouse system, with its sounds and signals coming from the shore, allowed the shipping industry to evolve smoothly, with the colonies reaping the benefits of increased trade. Today, lighthouses are scattered along the length of the Atlantic and Pacific coasts, as well as around the shores of the Great Lakes.

In 1716, the colony of Massachusetts built the first lighthouse in America in Boston

Harbor on Little Brewster Island. It was known as the Boston Light, and it was kept by George Worthylake, the nation's first keeper. It was also the first time a foghorn had been utilized in a lighthouse. The third keeper, John Hayes, asked that 'a great gun be placed on the Said Island to answer ships in a Fogg', consequently a cannon was used as the foghorn and was installed in 1719.

During the American Revolution, the original lighthouse was held by British forces and was attacked and burnt on two occasions by American forces, but as the British forces withdrew in 1776, they blew up the tower and completely destroyed it. The tower was rebuilt in 1783, and today the lighthouse is preserved by a special act of Congress to serve as a monument to the Lighthouse Service, ensuring that the traditions of lightkeeping will be maintained.

Onshore lights, or lighthouses built on land, made up the majority of the earliest lighthouses in America. These were made from a variety of materials and were in various architectural styles. Wood, stone masonry, brick, cast-iron plates, skeletal and reinforced concrete are some of the most common types of construction materials. Wooden lighthouses were common before the 19th century because wood was readily available, but were phased out due to danger of them catching fire. Masonry towers were made from rubblestone, cut stone, brick and concrete. The oldest standing masonry tower in the US is Sandy Hook Lighthouse (1764) in New Jersey. The original tower still stands,

LEFT: The Castle Hill Light is constructed from rubblestone.

OPPOSITE: The Roanoke Marshes Light is a screwpile lighthouse in North Carolina.

being octagonal in shape, with massive masonry walls that are 7ft thick at the base.

The screwpile lighthouse marked an important architectural development for lighthouses in the Chesapeake Bay area and along the coasts of the Carolinas. It was a type of offshore construction invented by Irish engineer, Alexander Mitchell, in the 1830s and was first used on the River Thames. It made its way to the Chesapeake Bay because of the estuarial soft bottom which allowed wrought-iron piles to be inserted for the lighthouse structure. Inexpensive to build, easy to construct and quick to build, it marked a significant improvement over the standard straightpile construction type.

The screwpile was normally a complex hexagonal structure that sat on six to eight outer piles and one central pile, all of which were then screwed into place. The first screwpile light in the United States was the Brandywine Shoal in the Delaware Bay, and screwpiles became especially popular after the Civil War when the Lighthouse Board approved a policy to replace lighthouses in the interior. Around 100 of these complex structures were built on the Atlantic coastline from the Delaware and Chesapeake Bays down to the Florida Keys and Gulf of Mexico. Other common types of offshore lighthouses included caisson, crib, pier/breakwater, and Texas towers.

One of the most famous of the screwpiles was the Thomas Point Shoal Light, built in the Chesapeake Bay, which has been called 'the finest example of a screwpile cottage anywhere in the world', its main purpose being to warn vessels that would require areas of deeper water among the shallow sandbars. Screwpile lights were especially vulnerable to storms and ice, which could cause the lantern to dismount or break, and for this reason Thomas Point is currently the

last remaining screwpile light in the Chesapeake Bay that stands in its original location. It was also equipped with a foghorn, something first used in the Boston Light. It remained manned into the late 20th century, at which point it was automated by the United States Coast Guard, something that happened to most lighthouses in the US as technology made it less essential for lighthouses to continue to be maintained by human keepers.

The waters of the Pacific North-West offer plenty of coastal diversity, while the Pacific Ocean and the estuaries of the coastal rivers mark an area of huge waves, high winds, towering cliff faces, rolling sand dunes and pounding surf. The ocean is busy with fisherman while the rivers are important to the region's lumber industry.

The coast of California is very rugged and often blanketed in thick fog, making it especially deadly for shipping. Lighthouses started to be built on the Pacific coast as settlers moved west in search of gold, although life for lighthouse keepers in that location could often be alarming experiences. Five keepers, for example, were kept at all times on the St. George Reef, because it was so difficult to operate, and their families were prevented from accompanying them. Weather conditions were often so treacherous that contact with the shore might be cut off for an entire month or more at a time.

A fine example of the lighthouses on the western coast is the Tillamook Rock Light, whose architecture has been described as a tremendous engineering feat and one of the most daring of the 19th century. Located 1.1 miles off the coast of Washington, it is isolated and located in an area where turbulent and stormy seas are commonplace.

The lighthouse took 575 days to build and cost one worker his life. Built on a rock, the

plans initially faced skepticism for being wasteful and foolish. Tons of rock had to be blasted away in conditions that included fog, rain and wind. To keep passing ships away during the blasting, the head of construction had to toss warning cartridges of exploding powder over the water.

LEFT: The Cape Blas Light was one of four towers, the previous three having succumbed to hurricanes and coastal erosion. This final steel structure, built in 1885, has stood the test of time.

OPPOSITE: The Block Island Southeast Light, on Rhode Island, is a most unusual red-brick structure.

CHAPTER TWO

LIGHTHOUSES OF THE NORTH-EAST

Annisquam Harbor Light

Annisquam, MA
Built: 1801, 1851 and 1897
Style: Cylindrical
No: 9615
Position: 42 39 42 N. 70 40 54 W
Focal plane: 45ft (14m)
Range: W 14 miles/22km, R 11 miles/18km
Height: 41ft (12.5m)

The first light station, a 40-ft (12-m) wooden tower, was established in 1801, but fell into disrepair and, in 1851, was replaced by an octagonal wooden tower of a similar height.

The original lighthouse keeper's house was repaired and, with alterations, has remained to this day. In 1869, a covered walkway was built between the house and the tower.

The original wooden keeper's house from 1801 is still used to house US Coast Guard personnel who manage the site.

In 1897, the current brick lighthouse was built on the same foundation as the previous two constructions. Some time after 1900, the covered walkway to the keeper's house was replaced by an uncovered wooden footbridge.

In 1931, a foghorn was installed, but until 1949, it was used only from 15 October to 15 May to spare summer residents the noise. The lighthouse was automated in 1974. The fog signal was first removed by the United States Coast Guard, but after complaints by fishermen and local boaters, it was re-activated and was also eventually automated.

The lighthouse was added to the National Register of Historic Places in 1987.

In 2000, a major restoration of the tower was conducted by the Coast Guard. In 2008, the building made an appearance, supposedly as a lighthouse in Maine, in the film remake *The Women* (starring Meg Ryan).

Barnegat Light

Long Beach Island, NJ
Built: 1835 and 1857
Style: Conical
Position: 39 45 07 N. 74 06 39 W

Barnegat Light, known locally as 'Old Barney', stands on the northern tip of Long Beach Island, on the south side of Barnegat Inlet.

The development of the original lighthouse began in June 1834, and the 40-ft (12-m) lighthouse was commissioned the following year, though mariners at the time considered the building's non-flashing, fifth-order light to be inadequate. Because of the strong currents in the inlet, the lighthouse was built 900ft (270m) away from the water; but within ten years this had dwindled to only 450ft (140m).

In 1855, Lt. George G. Meade, an Army engineer and later a Union general in the American Civil War, was assigned to design a new lighthouse. He was chosen largely because of his recent design of the åAbsecon Light. Meade completed the construction plans in 1855 and work began in late 1856. Because of continuing erosion during its construction, the new lighthouse was located about 100ft (30m) south of the original structure, the site of which is now submerged. During construction, in June 1857, the light in the original structure was relocated to a temporary wooden tower located nearby. This was prompted by the encroaching seas which threatened the original lighthouse and ultimately caused the tower to collapse into the water later that year. Because of the rough waters of the area, several jetties have been built throughout the history of both lighthouses.

The lighthouse was decomissioned in 1944 and is now a museum.

Bass Harbor Head Light

Bass Harbor, Mount Desert Island, ME
Built: 1858
Style: Tower connected to dwelling
No: 2335
Position: 44 13 19 N. 68 20 14 W
Focal plane: 56ft (17m)
Range: 13 miles (21km)

One of the most picturesque in the US, the lighthouse is situated within Acadia National Park on the south-eastern corner of Mount Desert Island, where it marks the entrance to Bass Harbor and Blue Hill Bay.

The history of Bass Harbor Head Light began in 1855 when it was deemed that sufficient reason existed for a lighthouse to be built at the mouth of Bass Harbor. $5000 was appropriated by Congress for its construction in 1858.

The construction of a fog bell and tower, which no longer remains today, was completed in 1876 with a much larger 4,000-lb (1800-kg) bell being placed inside the tower in 1898. The keeper's house has kept its original configuration with the exception of a 10-ft addition that was added in 1900.

Bass Harbor's fifth-order Fresnel lens was replaced in 1902 with a larger fourth-order. This lens was manufactured by the French company Henry-Lepaute, and remains in service today.

Today, the house is the private residence of a local Coast Guard member and his family. Tourists are able to get close to the bell and light via a concrete path, but most of the grounds remain private. There is a short walk which leads to a series of wooden steps and down onto the many granite boulders that provide great views of the harbour side of the lighthouse.

Bear Island Light

Bear Island, ME
Built: 1839, 1853 and 1889
Style: Brick tower

This lighthouse is situated on Bear Island near Mount Desert Island, at the entrance to Northeast Harbor, Maine. It was first established in 1839. The present structure was built in 1889. It was deactivated in 1981 and relit as a private aid to navigation by the Friends of Acadia National Park in 1989.

Bear Island has had three light towers in its time, the first being a rustic stone building, and the last, built on the site of the second tower 50 years later, is of brick construction. This 33-ft (10-m) tower, with a focal plane 100ft (30.5m) above the water, was fitted with a fifth-order Fresnel lens. The station was decommissioned in 1982 when a buoy took over the role of guiding vessels into the harbour.

Brant Point Light

Nantucket, MA
Built: 1746, 1759 and 1901
Style: Cylindrical tower
No: 15205
Position: 41 17 24 N. 70 05 25 W
Focal plane: 26ft (8m)
Range: 10 miles (16km)

Brant Point Light, located on Nantucket Island, was established in 1746, automated in 1965, and is still in operation to this day.

In the 18th century, Nantucket was a major centre for the local whaling industry, the island's geography providing a natural protected harbour for whaling vessels. The harbour entrance is bordered by Coatue Beach to the east and Brant Point to the west, and mariners also needed to navigate past the Nantucket Bar, two miles north-west of the harbour.

Brant Point Light was the second lighthouse to be built in the American colonies after the Boston Harbor Light. The first tower was destroyed by fire. The second, built in 1759, also caught fire several times, and was repaired by the Nantucket fishermen, who relied on its light to see them safely home. The wooden tower, that currently marks the approach to Nantucket, is the third such light, erected in 1901. It was equipped with a fifth-order Fresnel lens until it was eventually given a modern optic.

The light station was added to the National Register of Historic Places on 28 October 1987, and has the distinction of being the tenth light on the point, in addition to several range lights. Four of the others burned or blew down, two were condemned, two were unsatisfactory, and the remaining one stands unused.

Cape Ann Lights

Thatcher Island, MA
Built: 1771 and 1861
Style: Conical
No: 295
Position: 42 38 12 N. 70 34 30 W
Focal plane: 166ft (50.5m)
Range: 17 miles (27km)
Height: 124ft (38m)

Twin Cape Ann lighthouses have stood on Thatcher Island since 1771. The first 45-ft (14-m) colonial towers were replaced by the present 124-ft granite towers in 1861, but only the southern tower is active today. It was fitted with a first-order Fresnel lens until its automation in 1932.

In 1919, Cape Ann's foghorn saved the ship carrying President Woodrow Wilson home from Europe after signing the Treaty of Versailles. With the lights shrouded in fog, the captain of the SS *America* heard the horn at the last moment and was able to alter course in time to avoid crashing into the rocks.

The Cape Ann Light Station is nationally significant as the last to be established under colonial rule and the first station in the United States to mark a navigational hazard rather than a harbour entrance.

The current pair of lighthouses were built in 1861. They were both equipped with first-order Fresnel lenses, which stood approximately 10ft (3m) high and weighed several tons. The lens from the south tower is now in the US Coast Guard Museum which is at the United States Coast Guard Academy in New London, CT.

When these lights were built, there was no way to produce a flashing light and mariners would occasionally confuse one light for another with disastrous results. The only way to create a distinction was to build more than one light, there being two lights at

Plymouth and three at Nauset Beach. Gradually, as it became possible to create flashes with a revolving lens system, the multiple lights were discontinued, so that while the south light is active and Coast Guard-maintained, the north tower was discontinued in 1932. It was relit as a private aid to navigation in 1989. Both lights are now owned by the town of Rockport and managed by the Thatcher Island Association.

Cape Elizabeth Light

Cape Elizabeth, ME
Built: 1828 and 1874
Style: Conical tower
No: 7520
Position: 43 34 00 N. 70 12 00 W
Focal plane: 129ft (39m)
Range: 15 miles (24km)
Height: 67ft (20m)

Cape Elizabeth was given two lighthouses, one flashing, the other fixed, so that navigators could plot their position on a chart from any approach. The original stone towers, standing 900ft (274m) apart, were later replaced with the present cast-iron towers. They continued to operate in tandem until 1924, when the Coast Guard ceased to use twin lights. The keeper's house, from which Marcus Hanna went out in 1885 to rescue two seamen, is now in private ownership, as is the west tower. The 67-ft east lighthouse continues to operate.

The use of multiple lights in a given site was discontinued in 1924. The western light was removed from service, and eventually sold to a private party in the 1970s. The eastern tower remains in service.

Cape May Light

Cape May, NJ
Built: 1824, 1847 and 1859
Style: Conical, red-topped tower
No: 155
Position: 38 55 59 N. 75 57 37 W
Focal plane: 165ft (50m)
Range: 24 miles (39km)
Height: 157ft (48m)

The Cape May Light is located in New Jersey at the tip of Cape May in Lower Township's Cape May Point State Park.

It was built in 1859 under the supervision of US Army engineer William F. Raynolds, was automated in 1946, and continues to operate to this day. It is the third fully documented lighthouse to be built at Cape May Point, the first having been built in 1824; the second in 1847. The sites of the first two lighthouses are now underwater due to erosion.

There are 199 steps to the top of the lighthouse, revealing a view that extends to Cape May City and Wildwood to the north, Cape May Point to the south and, on a clear day, Cape Henlopen, Delaware, to the west.

The plastic lens that replaced the original first-order Fresnel lens has a range of 24 miles.

The lighthouse is the property of the state of New Jersey, after ownership was transferred from the US Coast Guard in 1992, which maintains it as an active aid to maritime navigation. The state of New Jersey leases the structure and grounds to the Mid-Atlantic Center for the Arts, which raises funds for the restoration and upkeep of the building and allows visitors to climb to the top. It has already spent $2 million in restoring the tower and turning it into an active museum.

Cape Neddick Light

York, ME
Built: 1879
Style: Conical tower connected to dwelling
No: 125
Position: 43 09 54 N. 70 35 30 W
Focal plane: 88ft (27m)
Range: 13 miles (21km)
Height: 41ft (12.5m)

Commonly known as the Nubble Light or simply, The Nubble, Cape Neddick is at the north end of Long Sands Beach in the village of York Beach. In 1874 Congress appropriated $15,000 to build a light station at the 'Nubble' and in 1879 construction began. Cape Neddick was dedicated by the US Lighthouse Service and began service in 1879.

There had been plans to build a lighthouse on the site since 1837. The tower is lined with brick and sheathed with cast iron. Although the tower stands 41ft tall, the light itself is 88ft (27m) above sea level because of the additional height of the site on which it sits.

Unusually, the stanchions of the walkway railing around the lantern room are decorated with 4-inch (100-mm) brass replicas of the lighthouse itself.

The brick-lined tower has an attractive wooden-framed keeper's cottage, with access to it by means of a covered walkway.

The lighthouse has been warning mariners of the dangers posed by Nubble Island (a barren outcrop of rocks off Nubble Point) ever since and it continues to perform this function to this day.

Cape Poge Light

Martha's Vineyard, MA
Built: 1801, 1844, 1880 and 1893
Style: Conical
No: 13715
Position: 41 25 10 N. 70 27 08 W
Focal plane: 65ft (20m)
Range: 9 miles (14.5km)

Cape Poge Light, sometimes called Cape Pogue Light, is at the north-eastern tip of Chappaquiddick, an island that is part of Martha's Vineyard off the coast of Cape Cod, Massachusetts.

There have been at least four towers on Cape Poge. In 1801 the first 35-ft (11-m) wooden lighthouse was built for $2,000. During the War of 1812, the light was extinguished for a few months and its apparatus hidden in the cellar of a Chappaquiddick house. This first lighthouse was moved in 1825 and again in 1838 due to erosion of the bluff on which it stood. In 1844 a new tower was built and it was supplied with a fourth-order Fresnel lens in 1857. In 1878, however, it was reported that the keeper's house would probably 'fall into the sea within two years', and a third lighthouse was accordingly built in 1880.

Finally, in 1893, the current white, conical, wooden tower was constructed 40ft (12m) inland from the previous one. The current tower has been moved four times, in 1907, 1922, 1960 and in 1987, when it became the first lighthouse to be moved by helicopter.

The lighthouse was automated in 1943. It was added to the National Register of Historic Places in 1987.

The Cape Poge Light can be seen in the final two shots of the film, *Jaws*, as Roy Scheider and Richard Dreyfuss swim back to the shore.

Castle Hill Light

Newport, RI
Built: 1890
Style: Conical
No: 17795
Position: 41 27 44 N. 71 21 47 W
Focal plane: 40ft (12m)
Range: 12 miles (19km)
Height: 34ft (10m)

Castle Hill Light is located on Narragansett Bay in Newport, Rhode Island, at the end of the historic Ocean Drive. It is an active navigation aid for the United States Coast Guard and boaters entering the East Passage between Jamestown on Conanicut Island, and Newport on Aquidneck Island, in Rhode Island state.

The architect, H.H. Richardson, made an early drawing for the proposed station. He was the designer of such acclaimed buildings as Boston's Trinity Church and the Buffalo State Hospital in New York.

The lighthouse was completed in 1890 on property formerly belonging to the famous naturalist, oceanographer and zoologist, Alexander Agassiz, of Harvard University. Agassiz sold land to the United States Government for the lighthouse for $1.00. After the hurricane of 1938, Mrs. Maximillian Agassiz, daughter-in-law of Alexander, sold the rest of the property to J. T. O'Connell, whose descendants are the current owners of the Castle Hill Inn and Resort.

Although the lighthouse is not open to the public, the shoreline and cliff face, on which the lighthouse sits, is accessible by means of several footpaths from the Castle Hill Inn.

The light has also been used, and still is, as a starting and/or stopping point in many regattas. It has a red light that flashes every eight seconds or so during the night.

Chatham Light

Chatham, MA
Built: 1808, 1836 and 1877
Style: Conical
No: 525
Position: 41 40 17 N. 69 57 01 W
Focal plane: 80ft (24m)
Range: 30 miles (48km)
Height: 48ft (15m)

The waters surrounding Cape Cod have a plethora of warning beacons – so many in fact that, in the early 19th century, mariners had difficulty identifying them. In 1808 officials conceived the idea of marking the busy channel leading to Chatham harbour with a double light.

The original wooden towers were built on a sandy ridge where erosion necessitated reconstruction in 1836. In 1877 the lights were replaced altogether by two 48-ft cast-iron towers fitted with fourth-order Fresnel lenses on the opposite side of the harbour. In 1923, one of these was dismantled and re-erected at Nauset Beach to replace the even rarer triple beacon known as the Three Sisters Light. The Chatham beacon is now illuminated through a modern optic.

Cuckolds Light

Cape Newagen, ME
Built: 1892
Style: Octagonal tower on dwelling
No: 5485
Position: 43 46 48 N. 69 39 00 W
Focal plane: 59ft (18m)
Range: 12 miles (19km)
Height: 48ft (15m)

The Cuckolds consist of two rocky islets rising about 15ft above high water in the westerly edge of the channel at the entrance to Boothbay harbour. They are dangerous, if approached on their southern side, on account of the reefs in that direction, and the shoals also extend half a mile westward of the western rock. The Cuckolds were much dreaded by mariners in bad or foggy weather and caused great peril to a large number of vessels.

In 1892, therefore, $25,000 was appropriated for the building of a fog-signal station and keeper's house. Because the rock is only about 15ft (4.5m) above high water at its highest point, it is washed by the sea in heavy storms. Therefore, a semicircular granite pier was constructed on the highest part of the island to support and raise the station structure above the stormy seas. The fog signal was a steam-driven Daboll fog trumpet.

The attached keeper's dwelling was a duplex made from a hard pine frame and was well-bolted to the ledge. It was attached to the fog-signal building. The dwelling consisted of a two-storey structure with cross gable dormers on the upper half-storey. The duplex was built so that one-half of the dwelling mirrored the other down the ridge of the roof. Each half consisted of a kitchen, pantry and sitting-room on the first level and two bedrooms on the second.

In 1902 a new oil-powered fog signal was installed.

A light tower was added to the station in 1907 due to a high frequency of accidents, despite the fog signal. Due to limited space on the island, the light tower was mounted on top of the existing fog-signal structure. The candlepower was 24,000 provided by an incandescent oil-vapour lamp and fourth-order Fresnel lens.

Deemed superfluous to the United States Coast Guard, and threatened with destruction, the Cuckolds was at a critical turning point in its history. In June 2004, under the National Historic Lighthouse Preservation Act of 2000, the federal government invited interested and eligible parties to apply for the acquisition of the Cuckolds Fog Signal and Light Station.

In August 2004, a small and totally committed band of local citizens began the arduous task of developing a plan to bring the Cuckolds Light back to its former glory.

Doubling Point Range Lights

Arrowsic Island, Bath, ME

Built: 1898

Style: Octagonal tower

No: 6135 (Front Light): 6140 (Rear Light)

Position: 43 53 00 N. 69 47 42 W

Focal plane: 18ft (5.5m)

The two wooden Doubling Point Range towers, standing 21ft (6.5m) and 13ft (4m) on Arrowsic Island, are the only examples of their type still operating in Maine. They help shipping pilots to stay in the safe but narrow channel towards Bath harbour. Navigators keep one light directly above the other. If one appears to slip to the left or right, they know immediately to steer in the opposite way.

Both towers were equipped with fifth-order Fresnel lenses, but these were replaced with modern optics when the lights were automated in 1979.

Doubling Point Light

Arrowsic Island, Bath, ME

Built: 1899

Style: Octagonal tower on pier

No: 6145

Position: 43 53 00 N. 69 48 24 W

Focal plane: 23ft (7m)

Range: 9 miles (14.5km)

The wooden lighthouse was one of a number of similar towers constructed along the Kennebec river during the late 1890s to guide shipping upriver into Bath harbour. It was originally equipped with a fourth-order Fresnel lens, which was replaced by a modern optic when automation occurred in 1988.

East Chop Light

Oak Bluffs, Martha's Vineyard, MA
Built: 1878
Style: Conical
No: 13745
Position: 41 28 13 N. 70 34 03 W
Focal plane: 79ft (24m)
Range: 9 miles (14.5km)
Height: 40ft (12m)

The cast-iron East Chop Light was built to guide vessels into Vineyard Haven. It is one of several historic light towers still in operation on Martha's Vineyard.

A semaphore station once operated at East Chop before the lighthouse was built, and this system was used to announce ships arriving at Nantucket between 1828 and 1834. A tower displaying a series of raised and lowered arms and flags also linked the site with stations in Nantucket, Woods Hole, Plymouth, Duxbury and Boston, among others.

There had been a lighthouse at West Chop, across the entrance to the harbour at Holmes Hole (the name was officially changed to Vineyard Haven in 1871) since 1817. A local mariner, Silas Daggett, lobbied for a lighthouse at East Chop, but the authorities apparently believed that a single light was adequate for the harbour. In 1869, Daggett took it upon himself to erect a lighthouse at East Chop. He operated it privately for seven years, receiving donations from local merchants for the upkeep of the light.

On 3 March 1875, Congress appropriated $5,000 for the lighthouse. The old structure was removed and a conical cast-iron lighthouse tower, 40ft tall, was erected in 1878, along with a one-and-a-half-storey keeper's house. A fourth-order Fresnel lens, with its focal plane 79ft above mean high water, originally showed a fixed light; it was changed to flashing red in 1898, and to flashing green in 1934. An oil house was added to the station in 1897.

In 1957, the Coast Guard sold the land surrounding the lighthouse to the town of Oak Bluffs for use as a park. The original Fresnel lens was replaced by a modern optic in 1984, and the following year, the Vineyard Environmental Research Institute became responsible for the maintenance of the lighthouse under a licence agreement with the Coast Guard. In 1994 the licence was transferred to the Martha's Vineyard Museum, along with the licences for the Gay Head and Edgartown Lights.

The grounds around the lighthouse are beautifully maintained. East Chop Light is open to the public on summer Sundays around sunset. For further information, contact the Martha's Vineyard Museum direct.

East Point Light

Maurice River, NJ
Built: 1849
Style: Lantern on dwelling

The East Point Light has played an important part in the maritime history of the Maurice river area of Cumberland County, New Jersey. Originally known as the Maurice River Light, it was erected in 1849 by the United States Lighthouse Establishment, the present name having been initiated in 1913. Throughout the years, its guiding light has shown fishermen, oystermen and recreational boaters the way into the mouth of the Maurice river and, during daylight hours, has been used as a landmark by hunters, trappers and surveyors.

Although numerous lighthouses once stood along the edge of the Delaware Bay, East Point is the last one remaining on the Jersey side. In fact, it is the second oldest lighthouse standing in New Jersey (only the Sandy Hook Lighthouse of 1764 is older). The lantern room offers a panoramic view of the surrounding land and water and is a favourite subject of photographers and painters alike.

The US Coast Guard operated the East Point Light from 1939 until 1941 when the light was extinguished due to the beginning of the war. In 1956 the property was deeded to the New Jersey Division of Fish, Game, and Wildlife. Over the years the vacant structure suffered greatly from vandalism and weather, but in early 1971 a group of concerned local citizens formed the Maurice River Historical Society, with the goal of saving the historic building from destruction. In July of that year, an incident occurred which nearly doomed the lighthouse; a trespasser in the building caused a fire which destroyed the roof and the lantern room.

In the mid 1970s, funded only by local fundraising and donations, determined members of the Maurice River Historical Society succeeded in rebuilding the roof and lantern room. Then, on 2 July 1980, at public request, the US Coast Guard reinstalled a beacon in the structure and put the East Point Light back on its list of active navigational aids.

Edgartown Harbor Light

Edgartown, MA
Built: 1828 and 1939
Style: Conical
No: 15420
Position: 41 23 27 N. 70 30 11 W
Focal plane: 45ft (14m)
Range: 5 miles (8km)

The original Edgartown Light was built in 1828 on a small man-made island in Edgartown harbour. An act of Congress allocated money to build it a quarter of a mile from shore. Later, $5,500 was appropriated to complete the project and Seth Vincent was paid $80 for a right-of-way to the tower. For the first year, the only way to get to the light was by boat, but another $2,500 was allocated to build a footbridge.

In 1937 the keeper's house, with its cupola-style light, was in poor shape, and the government announced plans to replace it with a steel tower. This proposal for 'navigational improvements' in the outer harbour inflamed the townspeople of Edgartown and there was a storm of protest.

Finally, a compromise was reached, and the Essex Light at Ipswich was dismantled and shipped to Edgartown on a barge in 1939. This is the tower which stands today.

Although the new light was placed on the original site, sand had filled in the area between the island and the mainland, and the current Edgartown Light now stands on the shore.

The island sits in treacherous seas, with one tide coming in from Boston, affecting the south side of the Vineyard, and another from Rhode Island, affecting the north shore. There are reefs, rocks and shoals, and the infamous Devil's Bridge off Aquinnah, which wrecked the steamship The City of Columbus on 18 January 1884, with the loss of 120 crew and passengers in the icy waters.

Nowhere, perhaps, is the notion of romance more firmly embedded than at the Edgartown Light. The light had originally been built into the roof of a 12-room keeper's dwelling on a man-made island a quarter of a mile offshore at the entrance to the Edgartown harbour. A long wooden pier connected the lighthouse to the shore. The wooden walkway became known as the Bridge of Sighs because it was where the young men of Edgartown took their girlfriends before they set off to sea on long whaling trips.

Erie Land Light

Presque Isle Peninsula, Lake Erie, PA
Built: 1818, 1858 and 1866
Style: Conical sandstone tower

The Erie Land Light, also known as the Old Presque Isle Light, is a 49-ft (15-m) lighthouse in Erie, Pennsylvania.

It was originally constructed in 1818 and was the first lighthouse to be built by the government on the Great Lakes. The lighthouse was a 20-ft (6.1-m) tall square tower and had begun to sink into the ground in 1851. It became necessary to replace the tower in 1858.

The second was a 58-ft (18-m) conical tower, whose foundation also proved to be defective, causing it to be replaced again in 1866. An investigation found that a thin layer of quicksand lay beneath the foundation of the tower.

The third tower was built from Berea sandstone, and to prevent the tower from sinking like its predecessors, 20-ft-long oak timbers were sunk into the ground with 6ft (1.8m) of crushed limestone and Portland cement poured over the timbers. A two-storey lightkeeper's saltbox house was also built at the same time.

The lighthouse was deactivated in 1880 when it was deemed superfluous because of the recently constructed Presque Isle Light on Presque Isle. It was sold for $1,200.

The government re-purchased and reactivated the light in 1885, after much public outcry, and it was operated until 26 December 1899 when it was again deactivated. The lenses were removed in 1902 and were sent to the Marblehead Light in Ohio, while a roof made from tarred paper was placed over the tower after the lantern room had been removed. The city of Erie bought the lighthouse in 1934.

Esopus Meadows Light

Esopus, NY
Built: 1839, 1872
Style: Octagonal tower on dwelling

Esopus Meadows Light, nicknamed 'Maid of the Meadows' and often simply referred to as the Esopus Light or Middle Hudson River Light, is a lighthouse on the Hudson river near Esopus, New York. The lighthouse stands on the west side of the channel, in the river, its granite foundation built atop piles that have been driven into the riverbed, making it accessible only by boat. Construction of the first lighthouse on the site began in 1838 when the land was ceded for $1.00 by the town of Esopus to the US government, which appropriated $6,000 to build the light.

The light became active in 1839, being a twin to the Roundout II lighthouse further north up the Hudson river. By 1867, however, the building had been heavily damaged by flood and ice and funds for a new lighthouse were allocated in 1870.

The current lighthouse was completed in 1871 and is the last wooden lighthouse in existence on the Hudson and the only Hudson lighthouse with a clapboard exterior. It opened for business in 1872, being one of a group of lighthouses in the north-east built to an award-winning design by a Vermont architect.

Esopus Meadows Light was closed in 1965 and by the 1990s had fallen into a state of disrepair. The most serious problem was the deterioration of the foundations, which had begun to fall apart due to ice damage.

The Save Esopus Lighthouse Commission leased the lighthouse from the United States Coast Guard in 1990 with a view to restoring it, eventually taking ownership in September 2002 as part of the pilot programme of the National Historic Lighthouse Preservation Act.

Fenwick Island Light
Fenwick Island, DE
Built: 1858
Style: Conical tower
No: 205
Position: 38 27 06 N. 75 03 18 W

Range: 8 miles (13km)
Height: 87ft (26.5m)

The Fenwick Island Light marks both the outer Delaware coast and the eastern end of the Mason-Dixon Line. The brick-built tower still has its original third-order Fresnel lens, but the keeper's house is now a museum.

The lighthouse is owned by the state of Delaware and maintained by the private, non-profit-making New Friends of the Fenwick Island Lighthouse.

Fire Island Light

West Islip, NY
Built: 1826 and 1858
Style: Conical
No: 695
Position: 40 37 57 N. 73 13 07 W
Focal plane: 167ft (51m)
Range: 24 miles (39km)

The Fire Island Light is a visible landmark on the Great South Bay, in southern Suffolk County, New York, on the western end of Fire Island, a barrier island off the southern coast of Long Island. The lighthouse is located within Fire Island National Seashore and just to the east of the Robert Moses State Park.

When built, the lighthouse was on the edge of Fire Island Inlet and marked the western end of the island itself. Fire Island, however, has extended itself through accumulating sand so that the lighthouse is now nearly 6 miles (10km) from the western end of the island at Democrat Point.

The current lighthouse is a 180-ft (55-m) stone tower that began operation in 1858 to replace the 74-ft (23-m) tower originally built in 1826. The US Coast Guard decommissioned the light in 1974. In 1982 the Fire Island Lighthouse Preservation Society (FILPS) was formed to preserve the lighthouse, and raised over $1.2 million to restore the tower and light.

On 25 May 1986, the US Coast Guard returned the Fire Island Light to being an active aid to navigation. On 22 February 2006, the light became a private aid to navigation. It continues to be on the nautical charts, but is operated and maintained by FILPS rather than the US Coast Guard. It was added to the National Register of Historic Places in 1981 and a boundary increase for the National Historic District occurred in 2010.

Five Mile Point Light

New Haven, CT
Built: 1805 and 1847
Style: Octagonal

Five Mile Point Light, also known as Five Mile Point Lighthouse or Old New Haven Harbor Lighthouse, is situated at the harbour entrance to Long Island Sound, five miles (8km) from downtown New Haven. It is located in Lighthouse Point Park.

A lighthouse was first established on Five Mile Point in 1805, but the original 30-ft (9-m) wooden tower was an inadequate navigational aid for vessels entering New Haven. It was not replaced, however, until 1847 by the present 65-ft (20-m) sandstone and brick octagonal tower, which was equipped with a fourth-order Fresnel lens in 1855.

The construction of a new lighthouse on Southwest Ledge, outside the harbour mouth in 1877, rendered the Five Mile Point Light redundant and it was deactivated.

Goat Island Light

Kennebunkport, ME
Built: 1835 and 1859
Style: Cylindrical tower
No: 8100
Position: 43 21 30 N. 70 25 30 W
Range 12 miles (19km)

The Goat Island Light can be seen from the shore in Cape Porpoise Harbor, just off State Route 9, north of Kennebunkport, or can be viewed by boat.

The lighthouse was the last station in Maine to retain a keeper, thanks to its proximity to President George Bush's family home on Walker Point, in that the present brick tower and Cape Cod-style keeper's cottage, dating from 1859, made an ideal security post.

The station was finally automated in 1990 when the original fourth-order Fresnel lens was replaced by a plastic optic.

Hendricks Head Light

Boothbay Harbor, ME
Built: 1829 and 1875
Style: Square tower connected to house
No: 5665
Position: 43 49 24 N. 69 41 24 W
Focal plane: 43ft (13m)
Range: W 9 miles/14m, R 7 miles/11m
Height: 39ft (12m)

The Hendricks Head Light was established at the mouth of the Sheepscot river in 1829, near to the part of Southport Island now known as Cozy Harbor and six miles from Boothbay Harbor.

Hendricks Head itself claimed the lives of the captain and crew of a schooner, wrecked there during a terrible storm in the 1860s. The lighthouse keeper, searching through the wreckage the following morning, found a baby girl, whom he and his wife adopted.

The first lighthouse comprised a granite keeper's dwelling with the tower on its roof. It exhibited a fixed white light which was changed to a revolving light in July 1855.

The first tower burned down in 1875, when the present tower and its attractive keeper's house was built to replace it.

Hospital Point Range Lights

Beverly, MA
Built: 1872 and 1927
Style: Pyramidal tower
No: 10000 (Front Light)
Position: 42 32 48 N. 70 51 24 W
Focal plane: 70ft (21m)
No: 10005 (Rear Light)
Focal plane: 183ft (56m)

Hospital Point Range Front Light is an historic lighthouse at the end of Bayview Avenue in Beverly, Massachusetts. It forms the front half of a range which guides vessels towards Salem Harbor.

The 45-ft (14-m) brick-built Front Range lighthouse is twinned with a second light set on the spire of a church in Beverly to keep vessels safely lined up through the narrow channel towards Salem. The Front Range tower was fitted originally with the uncommon three-and-a-half-order Fresnel lens, used more often on the Great Lakes, until it was replaced by a standard third-order lens.

Still an active aid to navigation, Hospital Point takes its name from a hospital once built on the same site to fight smallpox.

Established in 1872, the magnificent white brick pyramidal tower was built at a cost of $30,000 'to complete the lighting of Salem Harbor'. Interestingly, this same appropriation built not only Hospital Point but also lighthouses at Salem's Derby Wharf and Fort Pickering.

In 1927, Hospital Point became known as Hospital Point Front Range Light with the Rear Range Light being the steeple of the First Baptist Church, this being approximately one mile away, on Cabot Street, in Beverly.

The light was discontinued in 1933, and sold to a private individual, but it was reactivated in 1951 in response to increased boating traffic in the area.

Hyannis Harbor Light

Hyannis, MA
Built: 1849
Style: Conical

Tucked away on a side street, the Hyannis Harbor Light, also known as the South Hyannis Light, goes unnoticed by most of the tourists who come to the area to take a ferry to Nantucket or Martha's Vineyard, or to catch a glimpse of the Kennedy family's Hyannisport compound. The privately owned lighthouse and keeper's house have been altered so much through the decades that only an informed visitor would recognize what was once an important light station.

The original lighthouse was a mere shack, with a lamp and reflector borrowed from Point Gammon. Given that this was a busy harbour in the 19th century, the government decided to establish a lighthouse, this being a small, white tower at the harbour entrance in 1849. A keeper's house was constructed in 1850, and a Fresnel lens installed in 1856.

In 1885 a range light was added on the nearby Old Colony Railroad Wharf, this being a simple lamp hoisted to the top of a 20-ft (6-m) wooden tower. The new range light and the lighthouse would be lined up by mariners as a guide into Hyannis Harbor. Railroad cars would often be left in a position that blocked the range light, and keeper John Peak would have to remonstrate with railroad personnel until they moved the cars. The tower was rebuilt in 1886 due to the fact that the range light often extinguished itself during storms. An oil house was added in 1889.

The lantern room was removed and the lighthouse was decommissioned in 1929. It was sold to private individuals, who built an enlarged lantern room atop the tower for use as a sitting room.

Marblehead Light

Salem, MA
Built: 1835 and 1895
Style: Skeletal tower

Marblehead is a mecca, where sailing is concerned, and it is a picturesque town with many 18th-century houses and narrow, winding streets. Every year, crowds gather on Marblehead Neck to watch the passing sailboat races, and many have speculated how much more scenic this picture would be if the Marblehead Light had been a traditional lighthouse instead of a metal skeleton tower.

The harbour is situated between the main peninsula of the town and Marblehead Neck, a separate peninsula extending to the east. The neck is connected to the rest of the town by a long sand bar, now a causeway.

On 30 August 1831, citizens of Marblehead requested that a lighthouse be erected 'on the point of Neck at the entrance to the harbour'. Congress appropriated $4,500 for the lighthouse on 30 June 1834, and it was agreed that the northern tip of Marblehead Neck was the most suitable location. The station was constructed and put into operation on 10 October 1835.

The 1893 annual report of the Lighthouse Board made a case for a new, taller tower, prompting a request for $45,000 to be appropriated for the construction of a brick tower, around 100ft (30m) high, and the request was repeated the following year. Funds were eventually forthcoming, and a contract was awarded in June 1895 for the building of a new lighthouse, but it was not to be a brick tower. Instead, a 105-ft cast-iron skeleton tower was erected at a cost of $8,786.

This is the only lighthouse of its type in the New England states, the nearest similar tower being at Coney Island, New York. There are several of the same type in the mid-Atlantic region, however, and a few more in Florida.

The station was automated in 1960, when it was fitted with a modern optic.

61

Marshall Point Light

Point Clyde, ME
Built: 1832 and 1857
Style: Cylindrical
No: 4780
Position: 43 55 00 N. 69 15 42 W
Focal plane: 30ft (9m)
Range: 12 miles (19km)

Marshall Point Light Station was established in 1832 to assist boats entering and leaving Port Clyde Harbor. The original lighthouse was a 20-ft (6-m) tower lit by seven lard-oil lamps with 14-in (355-mm) reflectors.

The original tower was replaced by the present 30-ft (9-m) white brick tower built on a granite foundation in 1857, the tower being originally lit by a 5th-order Fresnel lens. A raised wooden walkway connects the tower to land.

In 1895, the original keeper's house was destroyed by lightning, and a Colonial Revival-style house was built to replace it. An oil house and a bell tower, with a 1,000-lb (450-kg) bell, were added in 1898. The bell was replaced by a foghorn in 1969.

The lighthouse was automated in 1980 and the original Fresnel lens was replaced with a modern 300-mm optic, the original lens being at the Maine Lighthouse Museum in Rockland. In 1986, the St. George Historical Society restored the keeper's house and established the Marshall Point Lighthouse Museum there, presenting the histories of the Marshall Point Light and other lighthouses nearby.

The lighthouse appeared in the 1994 film, Forrest Gump. The light station was transferred to the town of St. George in 1998 under the Maine Lights Program. The fog signal has been dismantled but the bell remains on display.

Montauk Point Light

Montauk, Long Island, NY
Built: 1797
Style: Octagonal, pyramidal tower
No: 660
Position: 41 04 15 N. 71 51 26 W
Focal plane: 168ft (51m)
Range: 20 miles (32km)
Height: 110ft (33.5m)

The Montauk Point Light is located in Montauk Point State Park at the easternmost point of Long Island, in the town of East Hampton, Suffolk County, New York. The lighthouse was the first to be built within the state of New York, and is currently the fourth oldest active lighthouse in the United States.

The tower was originally completely white, its single brown stripe having been added in 1899. A fourth-order fixed red range light was added to the watchdeck of the tower in 1903 to warn of the presence of Shagwong Reef, a navigational hazard about $3^1/2$ miles north-west of the lighthouse. The fixed light was severely damaged in the hurricane of 21 September 1938 and removed on 1 July 1940, when the lighthouse was electrified.

Mystic Seaport Light

Mystic, CT
Built: 1901
Style: Conical

Imagine a quaint town where time has stood still, a place that preserves the lost art of Americana and nautical heritage, and Mystic springs immediately to mind.

Mystic Seaport is already something of a movie star itself, the charming little village, situated a few miles from New London, Connecticut, having featured in *Mystic Pizza* as well as in *Amistad*.

Mystic's lighthouse is an exact copy of Nantucket's Brant Point Light. It is situated two miles upriver from Noank, at Mystic's whaling harbour, and is maintained by the Mystic Seaport Museum. The lighthouse is not an official aid to navigation.

Mystic Seaport has often been called a 'living museum', and it is notable both for its collection of sailing ships and boats, and for the re-creation of crafts and the fabric of an entire 19th-century seafaring village. It consists of more than 60 original historic buildings, most of them rare commercial structures that were moved to the 37-acre site and meticulously restored.

Nantucket Great Point Light

Nantucket Island, MA
Built: 1749, 1818 and 1986
Style: Conical tower
No: 13650
Focal plane: 71ft (22m)
Range: W 14 miles/22km, R 12 miles/19km
Height: 70ft (21m)

The first lighthouse at Great Point was a wooden tower built in 1749, which burned down in 1817. This was replaced the following year by a rubblestone tower, which survived for 166 years until it was blown down during a fierce winter storm in 1984.

Its replacement is a concrete and plastic replica, funded by a $2-million federal grant gained with the support of Massachusetts' late Senator Ted Kennedy, which was completed in 1986. The second lighthouse had been equipped with a third-order Fresnel lens, which was replaced with a modern plastic lens long before the tower was destroyed. The new tower has a solar-powered optic.

Great Point is now part of Coatue Wildlife Refuge. Much of the area is off limits because it is a nesting site for the endangered piping plover. There is an access fee to the reservation, and a four-wheel-drive vehicle is needed to negotiate the seven-plus miles over soft sand.

From May to October, the Trustees of Reservations present a daily natural history tour at Coskata-Coatue Wildlife Refuge. A naturalist guide leads participants on an over-sand vehicle tour, through the saltmarsh, to learn about the geology, ecology and history of the place and climb the Great Point Lighthouse.

Nauset Beach Light

Eastham, MA
Built: 1838, 1877, 1923 and 1996
Style: Conical
No: 510
Position: 41 51 36 N. 69 57 12 W
Focal plane: 114ft (35m)
Range: W 24 miles/39km, R 20 miles/32km
Height: 48ft (15m)

Nauset Beach Light consists of a cast-iron-plate shell lined with brick, and stands 48ft high.

The lighthouse station at Nauset Beach, built in 1838, had three separate light towers to distinguish it from the many others around Cape Cod, and consequently became known as the Three Sisters of Nauset. When it was threatened by erosion in 1923, one of the twin cast-iron towers at Chatham harbour was dismantled and re-erected here. In time, this, too, was threatened by the changing coastline, and in 1996, the 90-ton brick-lined, red-and-white tower was moved a second time, to a safer location farther from the cliffs.

The Coast Guard gave the tower to the National Park Service and the Nauset Light Preservation Society agreed to maintain it as a private aid to navigation.

New London Ledge Light

New London, CT
Built: 1910
Style: Cylindrical tower on brick building
No: 21825
Position: 41 18 18 N. 72 04 42 W
Focal plane: 58ft (18m)
Range: W 17 miles/27km. R 14miles/23km

The New London Ledge Light stands on the Thames river at the mouth of New London Harbor in Groton, Connecticut. It was originally called the Southwest Ledge Light, but it was felt that this would lead to it being confused with another lighthouse of that name in New Haven. In 1910, therefore, the lighthouse was given its present name.

The United States Coast Guard took over the running of the lighthouse in 1939 upon its merger with the Lighthouse Service, and the light was automated in 1987. In 1990 the light was added to the National Register of Historic Places.

This lighthouse is an oddity in that it resembles a three-storey French Second Empire mansion dropped into the middle of New London Harbor, having been built when the older New London Light was deemed to be inadequate. The small cylindrical tower, which rises from the mansion's roof, originally housed a fourth-order Fresnel lens which rotated in a pan of mercury, but this was replaced in 1984 with an automated beacon. This original lens was later put on display in the Custom House Maritime Museum.

The lighthouse has reputedly been haunted ever since the 1930s by the ghost of a keeper who leaped to his death from the ledge when his wife ran away with the captain of the Block Island Ferry.

The light can be viewed from Ocean Beach, or from the Block Island Ferry that passes nearby.

Newport Harbor Light

Goat Island, Newport, RI
Built: 1824, 1842 and 1865
Style: Conical stone tower
No: 17850
Position: 41 29 36 N. 71 19 36 W
Focal plane: 35ft (11m)
Range: 11 miles (18km)

The Newport Harbor Light (also known as the Goat Island Light or Green Light), is located on the north end of Goat Island, which is part of the city of Newport, Rhode Island, in Narragansett Bay.

A light has guided vessels passing Goat Island into Newport Harbor since 1824. The present 35-ft (11-m) granite lighthouse is the third tower on the site, built in 1865. It was equipped with a fifth-order Fresnel lens, which did not prevent an elderly submarine from slamming into the station and destroying the keeper's cottage in 1921. The Fresnel lens was replaced with a modern optic when the station was automated.

In 2000 the Coast Guard leased the light to the American Lighthouse Foundation; it is managed by the Friends of Newport Harbor Lighthouse.

Nobska Point Light

Woods Hole, MA
Built: 1828 and 1876
Style: Cylindrical
No: 15560
Position: 41 30 57 N. 70 39 18 W
Focal plane: 87ft (26.5m)
Range: W 13 miles/21km, R 11 miles/18km

Nobska Point Light or Nobsque Light, is located at the division between Buzzards Bay and Vineyard Sound in Woods Hole on the south-western tip of Cape Cod, Massachusetts.

Being so prominent, Nobska Point was an ideal place for a lighthouse, and Congress appropriated $3,000 for that purpose on 23 May 1828. The first lighthouse, built in 1828 for $2,249, was a typical Cape Cod-style structure with an octagonal lantern on top of the keeper's house. There were three rooms on the first floor of the dwelling, and two small rooms upstairs. The lantern held a lighting system of 10 lamps and 14-inch reflectors, displaying a fixed white light 78ft (24m) above the sea.

In 1876, the lighthouse was rebuilt as a 40-ft (12-m) cast-iron tower lined with brick, with a fifth-order Fresnel lens.

The tower still has its original Fresnel lens, displaying a red sector to those in danger of running onto the shoals, and a white sector to those in safe waters.

The light was automated and the Coast Guard keepers were removed in 1985. The last officer in charge was Charles Tebo, who lived at the lighthouse with his wife, Gina, and their two young children. After automation, the station became a home for the commander of the US Coast Guard Group Woods Hole, which was renamed in 2006 as Coast Guard Sector Southeastern New England.

Pemaquid Point Light

New Harbor, ME
Built: 1822, 1827, 1835
Style: Conical
No: 5145
Position: 43 50 12 N. 69 30 21 W
Focal plane: 79ft (24m)
Range: 15 miles (24km)
Height: 38ft (11.5m)

The historic Pemaquid Point Light Station is located in Bristol, Maine, at the tip of the Pemaquid Peninsula.

A lighthouse was commissioned in 1827 by John Quincy Adams and built that year, but due to poor workmanship (salt water was used in the mortar mix), the lighthouse began to crumble and was replaced in 1835.

The second contract for the construction stipulated that only fresh water be used. Keeper Isaac Dunham oversaw the construction and wrote in a letter to the US Lighthouse Establishment that the agreement had been upheld and that the work had gone well.

The present stone tower and wooden-framed keeper's house, standing nearly 40ft (12m) above sea level, date back over 150 years, though the first light station had been established at Pemaquid Point in 1822. The construction of light towers was in its infancy then, and it took three efforts to build a lighthouse strong enough to withstand the harsh Atlantic storms. The tower still has its original fourth-order Fresnel lens.

The keeper's house is now the Fishermen's Museum at Pemaquid, which contains displays and artifacts of the lighthouse and local maritime history.

The lighthouse is owned by the US Coast Guard and is licenced to the American Lighthouse Foundation.

Petit Manan Light

Petit Manan Island, ME
Built: 1817 and 1855
Style: Conical granite tower
No: 1735
Position: 44 22 03 N. 67 51 52 W
Focal plane: 123ft (37.5m)
Range: 19 miles (30.5km)
Height: 119ft (36m)

After a number of ships had been wrecked on Petit Manan Island during the early 19th century, a 53-ft (16-m) lighthouse was erected here in 1817. But its Winslow Lewis oil lamps were too dim to provide an effective warning and continued shipping losses prompted the construction of a second 119-ft granite and brick lighthouse in 1855. This still stands today, despite the strong winds that

visibly rock the tower on occasions. Its original second-order Fresnel lens gave the light a range of 19 miles, but this was replaced by a modern optic when the station was automated in 1972.

The light station is part of the Petit Manan Wildlife Refuge and is not open to the public. There is a colony of breeding puffins on the island – also boat tours to the island.

Point Judith Light

Point Judith, RI
Built: 1810, 1816 and 1857
Style: Octagonal
No: 19450
Position: 41 21 42 N. 71 28 54 W
Focal plane: 65ft (20m)
Range: 16 miles (26km)
Height: 51ft (15.5m)

The Point Judith Light is located on the west side of the entrance to Narragansett Bay, Rhode Island, as well as the north side of the eastern entrance to Block Island Sound. The confluence of two waterways make this area busy with water traffic and the waters around Point Judith are very cold and dangerous. Historically, even with active lighthouses, there have been many shipwrecks off these coasts.

Three light structures have been built on this site. The original tower, built in 1810, was destroyed by a hurricane in 1815. It was replaced in 1816 by a 35-ft (11-m) stone tower with a revolving light and ten lamps. The present octagonal granite tower was built in 1857. It is 51ft high which, with the height of its land foundation, places the focal point of the lens 65ft (20m) above sea level. The upper half of the tower is painted brown and the lower half white to make the lighthouse structure a more effective daymark for maritime traffic.

In 1871, ship captains asked that Point Judith's fog signal be changed from a horn to a whistle to distinguish it from the Beavertail Light, which used a siren to announce fog. A whistle could also be heard more distinctly over the sounds of the surf in the area. Point Judith Light was automated in 1954, and in 2000 underwent a major restoration, carried out by Campbell Construction of Beverly, Massachusetts.

Pond Island Light

Popham Beach, ME
Built: 1821 and 1855
Style: Cylindrical
No: 6025
Position: 43 44 24 N. 69 46 12 W
Focal plane: 52ft (16m)
Range: 10 miles (16km)

The Pond Island Light has marked the entrance to the Kennebec river and the port of Bath for 180 years. The existing 20-ft (6-m) cylindrical, white brick tower was built on a granite block foundation in 1855, replacing the original tower constructed in 1821. The lantern is black and houses a 250-mm, solar-powered lens which replaced the fifth-order Fresnel lens installed when the tower was built. The

1¹/₂-storey, wooden, Cape Cod-style keeper's residence, also built in 1855, was demolished when the light was automated in 1963.

The site is managed by the Maine Audubon Society, the lighthouse being part of the Pond Island National Wildlife Sanctuary. The station is open to the public from September through March each year but is accessible only by boat.

Portland Breakwater Light/Petroleum Docks Light

South Portland, ME
Built: 1855 and 1875
Style: Conical

The Portland Breakwater Light (also called the Bug Light) is a small lighthouse in South Portland, Maine, its flashing red beacon helping to guide ships from Casco Bay through the entrance to Portland. It was built in Victorian times when architects were encouraged to design public buildings as works of art.

It replaced an earlier tower, marking what was then a long breakwater defending the entrance to Portland Harbor. A land-reclamation project has led to the coastline engulfing all but the lighthouse, which was decommissioned in 1942.

The light was fully restored in 1989 and was reactivated in 2002. It appears as a private aid to navigation.

Today, the Bug Light Park allows visitors a closer view of the lighthouse, while being a memorial to the shipbuilding efforts that were a feature of World War II.

Portland Head Light

Portland, ME
Built: 1791
Style: Conical tower connected to dwelling
No: 7565
Position: 43 37 24 N. 70 12 30 W
Focal plane: 101ft (31m)
Range: 24 miles (39km)
Height: 80ft (24m)

Portland Head Light is an historic lighthouse in Cape Elizabeth, that sits at the entrance of the shipping channel into Casco Bay.

The lighthouse is one of the oldest structures in the United States. The stone tower, and its keeper's house, built on a rocky headland in what is now Fort Williams Park, caught the interest of President George Washington and marked the beginning of the process of political nominations of lighthouse keepers. A guiding light for vessels entering Portland harbour, the station's fourth-order Fresnel lens was replaced in 1989 with a modern beacon, and the house is now a museum where visitors can view the second-order bivalve lens that used to be here.

The station has changed little except for the rebuilding of the whistle house in 1975, due to it having been badly damaged in a storm. Today, the lighthouse stands 80ft above ground and 101ft above water, its white conical tower being connected to a dwelling. The 200,000 candlepower DCB 224 airport-style aerobeacon is visible from 24 miles away.

The grounds and keeper's house are owned by the town of Cape Elizabeth, while the beacon and fog signal are maintained by the US Coast Guard.

Portsmouth Harbor (New Castle) Light

Fort Constitution, New Castle Island, NH
Built: 1771, 1784, 1804 and 1877
Style: Conical tower with building attached
No: 8330
Position: 43 04 18 N. 70 42 30 W
Focal plane: 52ft (16m)
Range: 12 nautical miles (22km)

Portsmouth Harbor Light is located within Fort Constitution in New Castle, New Hampshire.

It is one of America's oldest stations, dating back to 1771 when a lantern swung from a pole on Fort Constitution. This was replaced by an 80-ft (24-m) wooden tower in 1784, which was rebuilt 20 years later. The present 48-ft (15-m) cast-iron tower dates from 1877. The fort and its lighthouse have had a number of notable visitors, the most distinguished being George Washington, the 'father' of the US Lighthouse Service, who took a tour of the lighthouse in 1789 and was so appalled by its condition that he fired the keeper!

The current light is a fixed green signal that is visible for 12 nautical miles. The light is made green by an acrylic cylinder that surrounds the lens.

Other structures at the light station that are still standing are the 1903 oil house and the 1872 keeper's house (currently United States Coast Guard offices).

In October 2008, the *Ghost Hunters* team of Jason Hawes, Grant Wilson and others investigated paranormal activity at the lighthouse, keeper's house, and Fort Constitution.

Prospect Harbor Point Light

Prospect Harbor, ME
Built: 1850 and 1891
Style: Conical
No: 1785
Position: 44 24 12 N. 68 00 48 W
Focal plane: 42ft (13m)
Range: W 9 miles/14.5km, R 7 miles/11km
Height: 38ft (11.5m)

The lighthouse is situated on Prospect Harbor Point, which divides Sand Cove from Inner Harbor at the head of Prospect Harbor, Maine.

The original granite lighthouse, attached to the keeper's house, was replaced in 1891 by the present 38-ft wooden lighthouse, with a fifth-order Fresnel lens, and a new 1$\frac{1}{2}$-storey keeper's house. The lighthouse has the appearance of a typical wooden-framed fisherman's cottage, but with a tower extending upward from its seaward wall.

The house and tower were at first attached by a covered passageway, which was later removed. A stone oil house was added in 1905, and for a time the station had an active fog bell.

The light was automated in 1934, but a keeper (John Workman) remained at the station until 1953. The Fresnel lens was replaced in 1951.

The light remains an active aid to navigation, while the surrounding grounds and buildings belong to the US Navy, the lighthouse being in the grounds of a naval installation. The keeper's house, known as 'Gull Cottage', is also available for overnight stays for active and retired military families, with active naval personnel receiving reservation priority.

The lighthouse was added to the National Register of Historic Places as Prospect Harbor Light Station on 14 March 1988.

Rockland Breakwater Light

Rockland, ME
Built: 1888 and 1902
Style: Square tower on fog-signal house
No: 1-4130
Position: 44 06 14.5 N 69 04 39.16 W
Focal plane: 39ft (12m)
Range: 56ft (17m)

Rockland Harbor Breakwater Light, which sits at the southern end of a 4,300-ft (1,310-m) breakwater which protects Rockland Harbor, was completed in 1902 and is owned by the city of Rockland, Maine.

There has been a lighthouse at Rockland ever since the breakwater was built there in 1888. The first tower was replaced in 1902 by a 25-ft (8-m) tower set on the roof of the keeper's two-storey house. The original fourth-order Fresnel lens has been replaced by a modern plastic lens.

The Coast Guard effected a major refurbishment in 1990 and, in 1999, transferred ownership of the structure to the city of Rockland. Since then, the building has been maintained by volunteers, while the light itself remains the responsibility of the Coast Guard. In 2003 a float and boat ramp was added.

Rose Island Light

Newport, RI
Built: 1870
Style: Octagonal tower on dwelling
No: 17857
Position: 41 29 42 N. 71 20 36 W
Height: 48ft (15m)

The Rose Island Light, built in 1870, is located on Rose Island in Narragansett Bay in Newport, Rhode Island. The Rose Island Lighthouse Foundation preserves, maintains and operates the lighthouse.

Rose Island is another of Narragansett's historic lighthouses to have been rendered redundant by the building of the Newport Bridge. Constructed in 1870, the tower rises from the roof of the keeper's house, which is in the then-popular style of the French Second Empire, and once held a sixth-order Fresnel lens. The station was decommissioned once the bridge had been opened, but the building has since been restored by the Rose Island Lighthouse Foundation to become a museum and guest-house. Its light has also been relit and is now maintained as a private aid to navigation.

For a fee to the foundation, visitors can spend a night as a guest or a week as the 'lighthouse keeper', completing many of the chores required to keep the lighthouse in good working order.

Sankaty Head Light

Nantucket Island, MA
Built: 1850
Style: Conical
No: 555
Position: 41 17 01 N. 69 57 54 W
Focal plane: 158ft (48m)
Range: 24 miles (39km)
Height: 70ft (21m)

The brick-built Sankaty Head Light, with its central red band, marks the 100-ft (30-m) cliffs on Nantucket's ocean shoreline. Erected in 1850, it was the first lighthouse in Massachusetts to be equipped with a Fresnel lens.

An incandescent oil-vapour lamp was installed in 1912, replacing the old wick lamp. The light was converted to electric operation in 1933, and its characteristic was changed to a white flash every 15 seconds.

A modern motor replaced the old clockwork mechanism that turned the lens, and the position of assistant keeper was thereafter abolished.

After a century of service, the Fresnel lens was removed in 1950 and was replaced by modern rotating aerobeacons. The old lens can now be seen at the Nantucket Whaling Museum.

In 1990, the Army Corps of Engineers estimated that Sankaty Head Light would be in danger of falling over the eroding bluff within ten years, and a move was estimated at $840,000. Concerned islanders formed Save Our Sankaty, a non-profit-making organization, to raise funds towards the move.

The move was completed in the fall of 2007, and the lighthouse was relit in its new location at the end of November. The new location is next to the fifth hole of the Sankaty Head Golf Course, 390ft to the north-west and 250ft from the bluff's edge.

Saybrook Breakwater Light

Old Saybrook, CT
Built: 1886
Style: Conical tower on cylindrical pier
No: 22495
Position: 41 15 48 N. 72 20 34 W
Focal plane: 58ft (18m)
Range: 11 miles (18km)
Height: 49ft (15m)

Saybrook Breakwater Light is located at Fenwick Point, at the mouth of the Connecticut river near Old Saybrook.

The lighthouse was erected in 1886 and stands at the end of a stone jetty to mark a sandbar at the mouth of the Connecticut river. The 49-ft cast-iron tower, built on a cylindrical foundation, is very similar to Connecticut's Stamford Harbor Light. It has a basement, four main floors, a watchroom and a lantern room. It was fitted with a fifth-order

Fresnel lens exhibiting a fixed white light with a red sector. A more powerful fourth-order lens was installed in 1890, but this has since been replaced by an automated plastic lens.

The lighthouse is also known simply as the 'Breakwater Light' or 'Outer Light', being one of two built off Lynde Point in the 19th century. The other lighthouse, known as the Lynde Point Light, or more commonly as the 'Inner Light', is 75 years older than the Saybrook Breakwater Light.

Scituate Light

Cedar Point, Scituate, MA
Built: 1810
Style: Octagonal
Height: 25 feet, 70 feet above sea level
Position: 42 12 18 N. 70 42 57 W

In 1810 the US Congress voted $4,000 to build a lighthouse at Scituate Harbor. The building, made of split granite blocks with a 1½-storey house attached, was activated the following year. The lighthouse provided mariners with a vital bearing when navigating near the dangerous Minots Ledge. The station was decommissioned when the second Minots Ledge lighthouse was completed in 1860.

In July 1991, the lighthouse was relit, but with the light visible only from land. A new 27-in diameter ventilator ball was crafted for the top of the lantern by local resident, Herb Jason, using a ball from the Sankaty Head Light as a model.

In August 1994, Scituate Light's comeback climaxed when the nation's 11th oldest lighthouse was relit as a private aid to navigation, the white light being visible for 4 miles (6km). At the relighting ceremony, Kathleen Laidlaw, of the Scituate Historical Society, remarked, 'The lighthouse has become almost the symbol of Scituate. The light will bring it back to life.'

By the early 21st century, it was realized that nearly 180 years of harsh New England winters had caused the bricks in the upper portion of the tower to deteriorate. In early 2004, spalling of the brick faces became clearly visible from the ground, indicating that the outer layer of bricks would have to be replaced, and this was completed in 2004. By June 2005, the tower had been repainted and was looking as good as new.

Sandy Hook Island Light

Sandy Hook, NJ
Built: 1764
Style: Octagonal
Position: 0 27 42N. 74 00 07W
Range: 19 nautical miles (35km)

The lighthouse stands just south of the entrance to New York City and the Hudson river and is located at the tip of Sandy Hook, New Jersey. It is surrounded by Fort Hancock and is part of the Gateway National Recreation Area.

The Sandy Hook Light is the oldest working lighthouse in the United States, having been designed and built in 1764 by Isaac Conro. At that time, it stood only 500ft (150m) from the tip of Sandy Hook; today, however, due to littoral drift, it is almost 1.5 miles inland from the tip.

The 85-ft (26-m) light was built to aid mariners entering the southern end of the New York Harbor. It was originally called the New York Lighthouse because it had been funded through a New York Assembly lottery and a tax on all ships entering the Port of New York. Sandy Hook Light has endured an attempt to destroy it (in that it was an aid to British navigation) by Benjamin Tupper, and a subsequent occupancy of British soldiers during the Revolutionary War. It has also withstood two-and-a-half centuries of storms.

The station was lit by a 48-wick open-panned oil lamp until 1857, when it was fitted with a third-order Fresnel lens that continues to project the light for 20 miles (32km).

The lighthouse was restored in spring 2000 as part of the Sandy Hook Unit of the Gateway National Recreation Area. During summer weekends, the New Jersey Lighthouse Society offers free tours every half hour from 12:00pm until 4:30pm.

Sea Girt Light

Sea Girt, NJ
Built: 1896
Style: Tower and dwelling
Height: 44ft (13m)

The Sea Girt Light marks the inlet leading to the Wreck Pond in Sea Girt, New Jersey.

The brick-built lighthouse, and its adjoining keeper's dwelling, which was the first in the United States to have a radio beacon installed (in 1921), remained in continuous operation until 1945. The station has since been restored by local historians, who equipped it with a copy of the tower's original fourth-order Fresnel lens.

At the outset of World War II, the light was deactivated and the lens removed; the house was remodelled to serve as a dormitory for a Coast Guard observation post. After the war, an aerobeacon was mounted atop the tower; but in 1955 the light was decommissioned and a beacon on a steel tower was erected on the lawn.

The lighthouse was offered to the state, but when it declined, the borough of Sea Girt purchased the lighthouse instead. It was used for the town library and for meeting space for many years, and in 1981 care of the building was taken over by the Sea Girt Lighthouse Citizens Committee, an independent non-profit-making organization dedicated to restoring and maintaining the lighthouse. This restoration was accomplished, and the building is now available both for tours and for a variety of meetings; the beacon was removed from the external tower and placed in the old lantern, now operated as a private aid to navigation.

Sheffield Island Light

Norwalk, CT
Built: 1828 and 1868
Style: Octagonal, integrated schoolhouse

The Sheffield Island Light is an historic lighthouse located at the southern end of the Norwalk Islands on the west entrance of the Norwalk river on northern Long Island Sound.

In 1826 the United States government purchased what was then known as Smith Island for the purpose of building a lighthouse, and Smith, the original owner of the land, served as the first keeper of the light which was completed there in 1828.

The first light originally ran on oil, and in 1857 was upgraded to a fourth-order Fresnel lens. In 1868 the original 30-ft (9-m) tower was replaced by a Victorian-style limestone (masonry) dwelling, with a 44-ft (13-m) light tower in the gable. The Fresnel lens from 1857 was moved into the new structure and, with a focal plane of 51ft (16m) above water, was visible for more than 12 miles (19km).

Greens Ledge Light was built to the west of Sheffield in 1900 and proved better located to warn ships of the rocks and shoals on the approach to Sheffield Island and Norwalk harbours, and the Sheffield Island Light was therefore deactivated in 1902.

In 1987 the 118-year-old structure was purchased by the Norwalk Seaport Association for renovation and restoration, and the lighthouse was placed on the National Register of Historic Places in 1989.

In 1993 an electric generator was added to the structure, but in the fall a great storm flooded the basement of the building and artefacts were lost or destroyed. In 2002 the Norwalk Seaport Association started a ferry service to the island, which is still in operation.

Spring Point Ledge Light

Portland, ME
Built: 1897
Style: Conical tower on cylindrical pier
No: 7610
Position: 43 39 06 N. 70 13 24 W
Focal plane: 54ft (16.5m)
Range: 11 miles (18km)

Spring Point Ledge Light is a sparkplug lighthouse in South Portland, Maine.

The lighthouse was constructed in 1897 by the government after seven steamship companies complained that many of their vessels ran aground on Spring Point Ledge. Congress initially allocated $20,000 to the lighthouse's construction, although the total cost of the tower ended up being $45,000, due to problems with storms and poor-quality cement. The lighthouse featured a fog bell, that sounded twice every 12 seconds, and a lantern fitted with a fifth-order Fresnel lens.

Improvements were made to the lighthouse throughout the 20th century. It was electrified in 1934, and in 1951, a 900-ft breakwater, made from 50,000 tons of granite, was constructed in order to connect the lighthouse to the mainland.

The lighthouse was originally owned and operated by the United States Coast Guard. On 28 April 1998, however, the Maine Lights Selection Committee approved a transfer of ownership of the tower to the Spring Point Ledge Light Trust, with the USCG retaining only the light and fog signal.

On 22 May 1999, Spring Point Ledge Light was opened to the public for the first time in its history. Today, it is a popular summer vantage and picnic spot for families and fishermen. Adjacent to the lighthouse, visitors may also tour the old Fort Preble, the Southern Maine Community College Campus, and visit a small gift shop.

Statue of Liberty

New York, NY
Built: 1886

The Statue of Liberty (Liberty Enlightening the World) is a colossal neo-Classical sculpture on Liberty Island in New York Harbor, designed by Frédéric Bartholdi and dedicated on 28 October 1886.

The statue, a gift to the United States from the people of France, is of a robed female figure representing Libertas, the Roman goddess of freedom, who bears a torch and a *tabula ansata* (a tablet evoking the law) upon which is inscribed the date of the American Declaration of Independence. A broken chain lies at her feet. Liberty is an icon of freedom and of the United States.

The 115-ft (35-m) copper-clad statue was the first lighthouse to be converted to electricity in 1916. It helped to guide ships in and out of New York Harbor until 1932, when the US Army fort on Bedlow Island, where the statue stands, was decommissioned. The island was subsequently renamed Liberty Island and the 225-ton statue was opened to the public.

Stepping Stones Light

Kings Point, Long Island Sound, NY
Built: 1877
Style: Square tower on stone pier
No: 21505
Position: 40 49 28 N. 73 46 29 W
Focal plane: 46ft (14m)
Range: 8 miles (13km)
Height: 38ft (11.5m)

Stepping Stones Light is a Victorian-style lighthouse in Long Island Sound, in Nassau County, New York. The lighthouse is square-shaped and made of red brick, standing 1$\frac{1}{2}$-storeys high, the Hudson-Athens Lighthouse being a virtual twin of this structure. The light is in current use, under the management of the United States Coast Guard, but it is not open to the public.

The name of the reef, upon which the lighthouse sits, took its name from a Siwanoy (Minnefords) Native American legend. According to the legend, the tribe used warriors, medicine and magic to chase the devil out of present-day Westchester County, New York, and onto City Island (formerly Greater Minneford Island), surrounding him at Belden Point. The devil then picked up huge boulders lying there and tossed them into Long Island Sound, using them as stepping stones by which to make his escape.

Stony Point Light

Stony Point, Henderson, NY
Built: 1826
Style: Square tower

The Stony Point or Henderson Light is the oldest lighthouse on the Hudson river. It is located at the Stony Point Battlefield in Stony Point, New York. It marked the entrance to the Hudson Highlands for nearly a hundred years and was built in 1826, the result of a contract between Thomas Phillips, of New York City, and Jonathan Thompson, Superintendent of Lighthouses.

The specifications called for the construction of 'an octagonal Pyramid, to be built of blue split stone and the best quick lime and sand mortar' to serve as a beacon for the increased river traffic created by the opening of the Erie Canal the previous year. The building plan stipulated that the tower be 20ft (6m) above the water table and have three storeys and a cellar for the storage of whale oil. A wooden stairway would lead from the first floor to the second, and a wooden ladder would connect the second floor with the lantern, the name given to the glass-enclosed top of the lighthouse. On 1 December, the lighthouse, complete with copper roof and ventilator, was finished, at a cost of $3,350.

In 1925 the original lighthouse was decommissioned and replaced by a steel light tower built near the shoreline. The light tower was manually operated until it was automated by the US Coast Guard in 1973. In 1986, the exterior of the lighthouse was repaired, painted, and the lantern reglazed. On 7 October 1995, the lighthouse, with an exhibit, a restored interior, and a period forth-order Fresnel lens, was reopened to the public and the light activated for the first time in 70 years.

Stratford Point Light

Stratford, CT
Built: 1822 and 1881
Style: Conical
Position: 41 15 17N. 73 10 33W
Height: 35ft (11m)

Stratford Point Light is an historic lighthouse in Stratford, Connecticut, located at the mouth of the Housatonic river. The first lighthouse at Stratford Point was a wooden tower, which was replaced by the present 35-ft brick-lined cast-iron tower in 1822.

In 1969, Stratford Point Light assumed a 'headless' appearance as the lantern was removed to make room for new automated DCB-224 aerobeacons. For a time, these powerful beacons made the light the most powerful on Long Island Sound. The old lantern was donated to the Stratford Historical Society, and it was displayed at Booth Memorial Park in Stratford for 21 years.

In 1990, a smaller optic was installed and the lantern was refurbished and reinstalled at a cost of about $80,000. The tower was repainted in 1996, keeping its distinctive markings of white with a brown band.

A Coast Guard family lives at the lighthouse and the station is not open to the public.

Watch Hill Light

Watch Hill, RI
Built: 1807 and 1857
Style: Square tower with attached house
No: 19795
Position: 41 18 12 N. 71 51 30 W
Focal plane: 61ft (18.5m)
Range: W 16 miles/26km, R 14 miles/23km
Height: 51ft (15.5m)

The Watch Hill Light, located in Watch Hill, Rhode Island, has served as a nautical beacon for ships since 1745, when the Rhode Island colonial government erected a watchtower and beacon during the French and Indian and Revolutionary Wars. Destroyed in a 1781 storm, plans were discussed to build a new lighthouse to mark the eastern entrance to Fishers Island Sound and to warn mariners of a dangerous reef south-west of Watch Hill. President Thomas Jefferson signed an act to build the lighthouse in 1806 and construction was completed the following year.

In 1827 a rotating light was installed to differentiate the light from that of the Stonington Harbor Light in Connecticut.

The square 51-ft granite tower, and the attached dwelling that stands here today, was completed in 1857, when a sparkling fourth-order Fresnel lens replaced the station's old lamps and reflectors. An automated modern lens serves the station today, and the keeper's house is a small museum featuring the station's original Fresnel lens.

West Bank Front Range Light
New York, NY
Built: 1901
Style: Conical tower on cylindrical base
No: 34790
Position: 40 32 18 N. 74 02 36 W
Focal plane: 69ft (21m)
Range: W 23 miles/37km, R 12 miles/19km

West Bank Light is in Lower New York Bay and acts as the front range light for the Ambrose Channel. It is currently active and not open to the public.

The tower was built in 1901 and heightened in 1908. The 55-ft (17-m) caisson-based lighthouse was adopted as the front range beacon to partner Staten Island Light when it was erected in 1912. This is one of the few lighthouses that is still equipped with its original fourth-order Fresnel lens.

West Quoddy Head Light

Lubec, ME
Built: 1808 and 1858
Style: Conical
No: 1040
Position: 44 48 54 N. 66 57 00 W
Focal plane: 83ft (25m)
Range: 18 miles (29km)
Height: 49ft (15m)

This is one of Maine's oldest stations, and marks the easternmost point of the United States. The original rubblestone tower was demolished in 1858, was rebuilt in brick, and was equipped with a third-order Fresnel lens. The candy-striped tower guides vessels into Lubec, while a separate building houses the station's automated foghorn. Earlier fog signals included a cannon, a 1,500-lb (680-kg) bell and a steam whistle. The station was finally automated in 1988 despite a vigorous campaign by its last lighthouse keepers.

The lighthouse grounds are now part of Quoddy Head State Park. In 1998, under the Maine Lights Program, the station became the property of the state of Maine. The light itself is still maintained by the Coast Guard as an active aid to navigation.

CHAPTER THREE

LIGHTHOUSES OF THE GREAT LAKES

Cana Island Light

Bailey's Harbor, WI
Built: 1870
Style: Conical tower connected to dwelling
No: 21255
Position: 45 05 18 N. 87 02 48 W
Focal plane: 83ft (25m)
Range: 25 miles (40km)
Height: 86ft (26m)

The Cana Island Light is located just north of Bailey's Harbor in Door County, Wisconsin.

It is currently used as an active navigational aid under the jurisdiction of the United States Coast Guard and as a museum. This lighthouse, along with the Bailey's Harbor Range Lights, was built to replace the Bailey's Harbor Lighthouse in 1869, and was first lit in 1870.

The lighthouse guides ships along the northern approaches to Bailey's Harbor. When the yellow brickwork began to erode in 1902, engineers encased the tower and its keeper's dwelling in steel, which continues to protect the structure. The station still has its third-order Fresnel lens, which is now automated. Today, the keeper's house is a private residence.

Cedar Point Light

Sandusky, OH
Built: 1839 and 1867
Style: Skeletal tower
Position: 41 29 17 N. 82 41 37 W

The Cedar Point Light is a restored lighthouse in the grounds of the Cedar Point Amusement Park in Sandusky, Ohio.

The original lighthouse at the site was built in 1839, and a front range light was added to the station in 1853. A new lighthouse, which is the structure which stands today, was completed in 1867.

The lighthouse served as a navigational aid until 1904, in which year the light tower was removed from the top of the dwelling. In the ensuing years, it was kept in use by the federal government as a buoy depot, a radio beacon station and as a search-and-rescue boat station. These last duties were transferred to the Marblehead Coast Guard Station in 1975, and the Cedar Point station was discontinued.

Cedar Point Amusement Park acquired the structure in around 1990, and spent the next decade refurbishing the dwelling and reconstructing the light tower. The lighthouse opened as part of a vacation cottage development in 2001.

Charlevoix South Pierhead Light

Charlevoix, MI
Built: 1885 and 1948
Style: Square tower
No: 17925
Position: 45 19 22 N. 85 16 11 W
Focal Plane: 41ft (12.5m)
Range: 12 miles (19km)

The first Charlevoix South Pierhead Light was built in 1885 to mark the channel between the little Lake Charlevoix and Lake Michigan. The original wooden tower was replaced in 1948, with a square steel tower, and was subsequently automated and fitted with a solar-powered optic lens. The land-based lighthouse keeper's residence was sold to a private owner and was demolished. The property became Hoffman Park, and all that remains is a metal plaque marking the spot.

In 2008, ownership of the lighthouse was transferred from the US Coast Guard to the city of Charlevoix and the Charlevoix Historical Society.

Chicago Harbor Light

Chicago, IL
Built: 1832 and 1893
Style: Rubblestone conical tower, floodlit
No: 19960
Position: 41 53 22 N. 87 35 26 W
Focal plane: 82ft (25m)
Range: 24 miles (39km)

The Chicago Harbor Light is an active, automated lighthouse, standing at the end of the northern breakwater protecting the Chicago Harbor, to the east of Navy Pier and the mouth of the Chicago river.

This was one of the first light stations to be built on the Great Lakes. The original lighthouse was constructed in 1832 to mark the mouth of the Chicago river and was replaced by a 48-ft (15-m) rubblestone tower complete with boathouse, keeper's quarters and fog signal. The present lighthouse was constructed in 1893 for the World's Columbian Exposition and was moved to its present site in 1919. Its third-order Fresnel lens was originally made for a lighthouse in southern California. The station was automated in 1979.

Eagle Bluff Light

Ephraim, WI

Built: 1868

Style: Square tower attached to dwelling

No: 21825

Position: 45 10 06 N. 87 14 12 W

Focal plane: 75ft (23m)

Range: 23 miles (37km)

Height: 43ft (13m)

The Eagle Bluff Light is located near Ephraim in the Peninsula State Park in Door County, Wisconsin.

Construction was authorized in 1866, but the lighthouse was not actually built until 1868 at a cost of $12,000. It was automated in 1926.

The lighthouse has a unique design that gives a keeper easy access to its tower. It is therefore ironic that it was automated in 1909, making it one of the first lighthouses able to dispense with a keeper. The keeper's dwelling is a yellow 1½-storey red-roofed building, on the corner of which sits the tower itself. Standing a total of 76ft (23m) above the lake, the light shone through a three-and-a-half-order Fresnel lens. The light has been a museum since the 1960s.

Eagle Harbor Light

Keweenaw Peninsula, MI
Built: 1851 and 1871
Style: Octagonal tower on red dwelling
No: 15195
Position: 47 27 36 N. 88 09 30 W
Focal plane: 60ft/18m, 18ft/5.5m
Range: W 29 miles/47km, R 22 miles/35km
Height: 44ft (13.5m)

The Keweenaw Peninsula was a prime mining area for copper during the mid-19th century, and the Eagle Harbor Light was built in 1851 to guide the ships into the harbour to load ore. The structure took the form of a rubblestone keeper's dwelling with a square white-painted wooden tower integrated into one end of the roof. The tower was capped with an octagonal wooden lantern with multiple glass panes, and was outfitted with an array of Lewis lamps with reflectors.

Twenty winters spent on the edge of Lake Superior took their toll of the tower and in 1871 the present brick tower was built in its place. The original fourth-order Fresnel lens continued to serve in the new lighthouse until it was replaced by an aerobeacon in 1968. The tower was finally automated in 1980.

Fairport Harbor West Breakwater Light

Fairport Harbor, OH
Built: 1925
Style: Square Tower with quarters in crib
No: 3870
Focal plane: 56ft (17m)
Range: 17 miles (27km)
Height: 10ft (3m)

The Fairport Harbor West Breakwater Light, on Lake Erie, is located near the end of the western breakwater at the mouth of the Grand river. It was built in 1925, replacing the Grand River (Fairport Harbor) Light, which still stands and is now in a marine museum.

The white brick tower stands squarely on its concrete pierhead. With its red roof and period windows, with shutters marking its flanks, the tower, now automated, still holds its original fourth-order Fresnel lens.

The light is closed to the public. However, it is possible to walk out along the breakwater to view the structure and the grounds.

In 2006, an effort was begun by a group of community activists to take ownership of the lighthouse with the goal of preserving the facility for future generations.

The lighthouse will be sold by auction, although the United States Coast Guard will continue to maintain the light and foghorn as navigational aids.

Grand Haven Pier Lights

Grand Haven, MI
Built: 1895 and 1905
Style: Cylindrical tower and square building
No: 18965
Position: 43 03 25 N. 86 15 22 W
Focal plane: 42ft (13m)
Range: 13 miles (21km)

South Pierhead Inner Light

No: 18975
Focal plane: 52ft (16m)
Range: 16 miles (26km)
Height: 51ft (15.5m)

These striking lighthouses stand at the entrance to Grand Haven river, one of Michigan's deepest harbours. The inner light is a red-painted steel tower equipped with a sixth-order Fresnel lens. The wooden Pier Light was once a foghorn tower; it was moved to its present location and encased in iron plates when the pier was extended in 1905.

Grand Traverse Light

Northport, MI
Built: 1852 and 1858
Style: Square tower and integrated dwelling

Grand Traverse Light is located at the tip of the Leelanau Peninsula, which separates Lake Michigan and Grand Traverse Bay. It marks the Manitou Passage, where Lake Michigan elides into Grand Traverse Bay.

In 1858, the present light was built, replacing a separate round tower built in 1852. The lighthouse is located inside Leelanau State Park, 8 miles (13km) north of Northport, a town of about 650 people. This area, in the Michigan wine country, is known for its exquisite beauty and is a popular spot for tourists during the summer months.

Built on Cat Head Point, the Grand Traverse lighthouse, with its imposing brick-built two-storey keeper's house, guided vessels into Grand Traverse. Fitted with a fourth-order Fresnel lens, the lighthouse served mariners for 119 years until it was decommissioned in 1972.

Today, the station is now a lighthouse museum, with the restored lighthouse arranged to resemble a keeper's home of the 1920s and 1930s. Exhibits of area lighthouses, foghorns, shipwrecks and local history are located in the Lighthouse and Fog Signal Building. The restored air diaphone foghorn is demonstrated throughout the year, and visitors can climb the tower for a spectacular view of Lake Michigan. An admission fee is charged.

Grosse Point Light

Evanston, IL
Built: 1873
Style: Conical brick tower
No: 7-20190
Focal plane: 119ft (36m)
Height: 113ft (34m)

The historic Grosse Point Light is located in Evanston, Illinois.

The United States government agreed to construct the lighthouse at Grosse Point after several maritime disasters near the area demonstated a need for it. Shoals were a real hazard, and ship traffic was increasing, concurrent with development in the Midwest, the growth of Chicago, the aftermath of the Chicago Fire, and the increased trade and exploitation of natural resources throughout the Great Lakes. Particularly influential was the 1860 sinking of the *Lady Elgin*, a disaster which purportedly claimed up to 400 lives.

The citizens of Evanston petitioned the government for the light station during the Civil War but the project was delayed. Earlier lighthouses in Chicago proper, however, were proving themselves ineffective, so there was a perceived need for renewed action.

Grosse Point Light is one of the highest towers on the Great Lakes. Built in 1873, the brick lighthouse, with its extensive keeper's dwelling, fog-signal house and outbuildings, was given a second-order Fresnel lens – the most powerful light on the Great Lakes. Grosse Point was decommissioned in 1935 but has since been fully restored.

The light station is located at 2601 Sheridan Road, at the corner of Central Street. A small admission fee is charged. Next door, and to the north, the Evanston Art Center has free parking that is available to visitors.

Holland Harbor Light

Holland, MI
Built: 1872 and 1936
Style: Square tower

The Holland Harbor Light is located in Ottawa County, Michigan, at the entrance of a channel connecting Lake Michigan with Lake Macatawa, and gives access to the city of Holland

The first Holland Harbor lighthouse to shine out over Black Lake was built in 1872 but eventually succumbed to harsh winter storms and ice, so its 1936 replacement was sheathed in steel to provide it with additional protection.

The tower rises from the substantial keeper's dwelling, the whole structure being painted red – hence its nickname, 'Big Red'. Holding a sixth-order Fresnel lens, the US Coast Guard then recommended that it be abandoned in 1970, and citizens circulated petitions to rescue it. The Holland Harbor Lighthouse Historical Commission was then organized to preserve and restore this important landmark.

Except for its colour, Holland Harbor is a virtual twin of the Kewaunee Pierhead Light on the Wisconsin side of Lake Michigan.

In 2007, the United States Department of the Interior announced that the Holland Harbor Light would be protected, making it the 12th Michigan lighthouse to be accorded such status.

Public access to Big Red is somewhat limited due to the fact that it is necessary to cross private property to see the lighthouse up close, although there are no barriers to walking into the lighthouse area. The best vantage points, that are easily accessible to the general public, are from across the channel at Holland State Park.

Little Sable Point Light

Mears, MI
Built: 1874
Style: Conical brick tower
No: 18645
Position: 43 39 09 N. 86 32 24 W
Focal plane: 108ft (33m)
Range: 17 miles (27km)
Height: 107ft (33m)

The Little Sable Point Light is located south of Pentwater in the lower peninsula of the state of Michigan. It is in the south-west corner of Golden Township, just south of the Silver Lake State Park.

This lighthouse was to be the model for its nearby sister tower, completed two years later on Big Sable Point. The two towers are both 107ft high, built of brick, and were each fitted with third-order Fresnel lenses.

The difference between them now is that while Little Sable remains very much as it was built, its sister tower has had to be encased in ironwork to prevent it from falling down.

Little Sable was automated in 1954 when the keeper's dwelling and outhouses were demolished. The 39 acres of the original station are now part of the Silver Lake State Park.

Lorain Light

Lorain, OH
Built: 1837 and 1917
Style: Caisson

The Lorain Light began life as a simple lantern hung on the end of a pole to mark the Lorain shoreline of Lake Erie.

In 1837 the first wooden lighthouse was constructed on the end of a pier, but it burned too much soot, and in 1917 the Army Corps of Engineers was given the task of constructing the present stone lighthouse and two-storey dwelling on a giant concrete-filled caisson to withstand the worst of the storms and ice that badly effect Lake Erie during the winter.

This was equipped with a rotating fourth-order Fresnel lens to give the station a range of 15 miles (24km). The Lorain Light was finally decommissioned in 1965 and five years were spent raising $850,000 to save the landmark from demolition. The light was listed on the National Register of Historic Places in December 1978.

Mackinac (Old) Point Light

Mackinaw City, MI
Built: 1892
Style: Cylindrical with attached dwelling

The Straits of Mackinac had been a significant hazard to waterborne travellers even before the advent of European explorers. Consequently, before lighthouses came to be built, the Ojibwa used to light fires along the shore.

Mackinaw Point marks the junction of Lakes Michigan and Huron. Built in 1892, the 40-ft (12-m) Mackinac Point Light, and its castellated dwelling, continued in service until 1957, when the station was made obsolete by a bridge built over the Mackinac Strait. Since the Mackinac Bridge has lights on it at night, the bridge became a much better aid to navigation than the lighthouse itself.

In 1960, the lighthouse property was purchased by the Mackinac Island State Park Commission, which incorporated the lighthouse into the surrounding Michilimackinac State Park.

In 2000, work was undertaken with the intention of restoring the lighthouse, with its castle-like structure unique to the Great Lakes, to the way it looked in around 1910. The lighthouse complex, including the lightkeeper's quarters and tower, was reopened to the public in 2004.

The building is now used as an information centre and maritime museum within an historic park.

The lighthouse's original Fresnel lens is on display to the public, although an admission fee is charged.

Manitowoc Light

Manitowoc, WI
Built: 1840, 1895 and 1918
Style: Cylindrical tower on house
Position: 44 5 34 N. 87 38 37 W

The Manitowoc North Breakwater Light is located at the mouth of the Manitowoc river on Lake Michigan in Manitowoc, Wisconsin. It was built in 1918 to replace earlier lights built in 1840 and 1895.

The steel-framed, white fog-signal building, with steel tower on top, rests on a 22- x 48-ft (7- x 15-m) concrete crib. The first floor measures 19 x 34ft (6 x 10.4m) and serves as the compressor room. The second floor watchroom is 17ft^2 and supports a round light tower 12ft (4m) in diameter and a ten-sided lantern.

In 1840 a brick structure at the mouth of the Manitowoc river was in operation and in 1850 a wooden pyramidal tower was located at the outer end of pier. The 1840 tower was demolished and replaced in 1895. The 1850 Pierhead Light was destroyed during a storm in 1937 and was replaced with a skeletal tower.

Overall, the current structure is 40ft (12m) high and creates a focal plane 51ft (15.5m) above the mean low water level of Lake Michigan. The present lens is a fifth-order Fresnel made by Sautter, Lemonnier & Co. of Paris. The current lens replaced an original 1918 fourth-order Fresnel lens.

The light is located on the north breakwater, along Maritime Drive in downtown Manitowoc, behind the Manitowoc Maritime Museum. It can also be viewed from the southern breakwater, near the Lake Michigan SS Badger car ferry dock.

The light is an active aid to navigation and is not open to the public.

Marblehead Light

Bay Point, OH
Built: 1821
Style: Conical tower
No: 5250
Position: 41 32 12 N. 82 42 42 W
Focal Plane: 67ft (20.5m)
Height: 65ft (20m)

Located in Marblehead, Ohio, the Marblehead Light is the oldest lighthouse in continuous operation on the United States side of the Great Lakes. It has guided sailors safely along the rocky shores of the Marblehead Peninsula since 1822, and is an active aid to navigation.

The conical stone tower has changed little over the years except for its light. Originally, this was powered by 13 oil lamps, which were replaced first by a fourth-order Fresnel lens, and in 1903 by the present third-order system.

The beacon was automated in 1958. Today's 300-mm lens projects a green signal that flashes every six seconds and is visible for 11 nautical miles (20 km). The distinctive green distinguishes the lighthouse signal from white lights coming from air beacons.

With its original finish tattered by time and harsh weather, the exterior of the lighthouse tower was given a fresh coat of stucco the same year that the beacon was automated. The US Coast Guard continues to operate and maintain the lighthouse beacon.

The Ohio Department of Natural Resources has maintained the property surrounding the lighthouse since 1972 and accepted ownership of the Marblehead Light tower in May 1998.

The keeper's cottage now houses a museum managed by the Ottawa County Historical Society.

Michigan City East Pier Light

Michigan City, IN
Built: 1904
Style: Octagonal tower attached to building
No: 19545
Position: 41 43 42 N. 86 54 42 W

Range: 12 miles (19km)
Height: 49ft (15m)

The lighthouse was built in 1904 to guide vessels into the city harbour. Constructed on a square concrete platform, the octagonal tower has a pyramid-shaped roof above the lantern and is sheathed in steel to protect it from storms. The station houses a fog signal and a rotating 2130c optic lens, which replaced its fifth-order Fresnel lens when the tower was automated in 1960.

Milwaukee Breakwater Light

Milwaukee, WI
Built: 1926
Style: Black lantern on square structure
No: 20635
Position: 43 01 37 N. 87 52 55 W
Focal plane: 61ft (19m)
Range: 19 miles (31km)
Height: 53ft (16m)

The Milwaukee Breakwater Light is located in the harbour of Milwaukee in Milwaukee County, Wisconsin. It protects the entrance to the Milwaukee river. The structure is near to the middle of the four-mile-long (6.4-m) Milwaukee breakwater.

The lighthouse was built in 1926 to guide vessels into the port. Fitted with a fourth-order Fresnel lens, the station was automated in 1966. It is built to withstand the heavy weather and waves when Lake Michigan is at its roughest.

The building is made of quarter-inch steel plates over a steel skeleton frame, and is equipped with windows and portholes with glass a full half an inch thick. The structure was originally painted red, but has remained white thereafter.

Muskegon South Pier Light

Muskegon, MI
Built: 1903
Style: Conical
No: 18710
Position: 43 13 36 N. 86 20 29 W
Focal plane: 50ft (15m)
Range: 15 miles (24km)
Height: 48ft (15m)

The Muskegon South Pier Light is located in the harbour of Muskegon, Michigan.

The narrow strip of water that connects Muskegon Lake to Lake Michigan is protected by two concrete walls and the Muskegon South Breakwater Light stretching out into the water. Between the two breakwaters, the Muskegon South Pier Light sits on a short pier on the south side of the channel mouth.

The first lighthouse in Muskegon consisted of a wooden tower atop the keeper's quarters built in 1851. It was situated on land. In 1871 the Muskegon Breakwater Light was built on the end of the breakwater and the main light was rebuilt. Muskegon Pier Light was built in 1903, replacing the main light.

The tower houses a fourth-order Fresnel lens and continues to guide ships across the passage between Muskegon Lake and Lake Michigan.

In 2008 the lighthouse became available for transfer under the National Historic Lighthouse Preservation Act, and in June 2010 ownership was transferred to the Michigan Lighthouse Conservancy.

The site is accessible but the lighthouse is closed to the public.

New Presque Isle Light

Presque Isle, MI
Built: 1840 and 1871
Style: Conical

Presque Isle boasts no less than four lighthouses within a 100-acre (40-hectare) park. The first light was the Old Presque Isle, a 30-ft (9-m) white, conical tower dating back to 1840. During the Civil War, the port was equipped with front and rear range lights to mark the channel into Presque Isle harbour, and a year later the Old Presque Isle was decommissioned. This was replaced by the present 113-ft (34.5-m) New Presque Isle Light, which remains one of the tallest on the Great Lakes. This was fitted with a third-order Fresnel lens, giving the light a range of 25 miles (40km). It was automated in 1970 and is now managed by the Presque Isle Historical Society.

Point Betsie Light

Frankfort, MI
Built: 1858
Style: Cylindrical tower attached to dwelling
No: 18370
Position: 44 41 29 N. 86 15 19 W
Focal plane: 52ft (16m)
Range: 19 miles (30.5km)
Height: 37ft (11m)

Point Betsie Light is located on the north-east shore of Lake Michigan, at the southern entrance to the Manitou Passage, north of Frankfort in Benzie County in northern Michigan.

The lighthouse was built in 1858 to guide vessels in and out of the Manitou Passage, and it remains one of the most important navigational aids on the Great Lakes. The plan for the lighthouse stipulated a cylindrical single-walled tower constructed of cream city brick, standing 37ft in height from the foundation to the top of the ventilator ball. Fitted with a fourth-order Fresnel lens, the tower was one of the last in the area to be automated, its resident keepers maintaining a watchful eye on shipping movements until 1983. The house is now a private residence.

The station was transferred to Benzie County under the terms of the National Historic Lighthouse Preservation Act in 2004.

It has been repainted according to its original colour scheme, which had not been seen since the 1940s. The Friends of Point Betsie Lighthouse have undertaken a complete restoration of the station.

Point Betsie is said to be one of America's most photographed lighthouses, and the most visited attraction in Benzie County. Because of its picturesque form and location, it is often the subject of photographs and drawings.

Point Iroquois Light

Brimley, MI
Built: 1855 and 1871
Style: Conical tower

Point Iroquois Light is located on a Chippewa County bluff in the state of Michigan. Point Iroquois and its light mark the division line between Whitefish Bay and the western end of the St. Mary's river, which connects Lake Superior and other Great Lakes.

The 65-ft (20-m) conical brick lighthouse was built in 1871 to replace the previous wooden tower dating back to 1855. The light, which was automated in 1962 and decommissioned nine years later, guided vessels through the hazardous reefs at Gross Cap and on into the St. Mary's river. The station is now owned by the Bay Mills-Brimley Historical Research Society, and houses a museum.

Port Sanilac Light

Port Sanilac, MI
Built: 1886
Style: Octagonal tower
No: 10115
Position: 43 25 48 N. 82 32 24 W
Focal plane: 69ft (21m)
Range: 16 miles (26km)
Height: 59ft (18m)

Port Sanilac Light is a United States Coast Guard lighthouse located on Point Sanilac, near Port Sanilac on the eastern side of

Michigan's Thumb. It is an automated and active aid to navigation on Lake Huron.

The lighthouse, positioned at the mouth of the St. Clair river, was built in 1886 as part of a 300-mile (480-km) chain of beacons designed to guide vessels along Michigan's eastern shoreline.

The original fourth-order Fresnel lens is still operational, being one of only 70 such lenses that remain active in the United States; 16 of them are in use on the Great Lakes, eight of which are in Michigan.

The Port Sanilac Light complex currently

consists of five historic structures. In addition to the light tower and ornate brick lighthouse keeper's residence, which is now a private home, the brick oil house, wooden outhouse and well also survive, the well being covered by a safety platform of wooden planks.

Located on private property, access to the lighthouse and its surroundings is prohibited. Viewing from the parking lot is good, and it is also possible to walk down towards the beach and breakwater to get a better view of the lighthouse and harbour.

Rawley Point Light

Two Rivers, WI
Built: 1853, 1874 and 1894
Style: Skeletal tower
No: 20935
Position: 44 12 42 N. 87 30 30 W
Focal plane: 113ft (34m)
Range: 34 miles (55km)
Height: 111ft (34m)

The first Rawley Point light station was established in 1853 to warn vessels away from a hazardous shoal. This, in turn, was superseded in 1894 by the present 111-ft skeletal tower, which was known locally as the Twin River Point Light, later the Rawley Point Light. The skeletal frame has a 6-ft diameter cylinder for stairs. This cast-iron structure, with its eight bracing legs, was fitted with a third-order Fresnel lens.

Other lights at this site included a wooden tower in 1853, and a square brick tower in 1874, the two-storey keeper's house having been built at the same time. Before the new lighthouse was built, 26 ships had foundered or had been stranded on the point. They included 20 schooners, a barge, two steamers and three brigs. The most tragic sinking in the point's troubled history occurred in 1887, when the steamship *Vernon* went down in heavy seas. One of the largest steamers on the lakes at the time, the *Vernon* took 36 crew members and passengers to their deaths. The sinking remains a mystery.

The light's Fresnal lens was replaced with an aeromarine beacon when the tower was automated in 1979.

Today, the site is a US Coast Guard residence within a state park. Views of the light can be obtained from the surrounding beach area, but the house and grounds are not open to the public.

Sand Hills Light

Eagle River, MI
Built: 1917
Style: Square tower and integrated building

The Sand Hills Light is located on the shore of Lake Superior in Ahmeek, on the Keweenaw Peninsula in Keweenaw County, Michigan.

The 91-ft (28-m) lighthouse was built in 1917 to mark the entrance to the Eagle river. The tower, which has a large keeper's house attached, was equipped with a fourth-order Fresnel lens, which was transferred to the Dossin Great Lakes Museum in Detroit when the station was automated in 1939.

The site then became a US Coast Guard training centre until the station was decommissioned in 1954, due, in part, to improvements in weather forecasting and the adoption of radar.

The lighthouse remained idle and unoccupied for the next few years, until it was finally sold at public auction to H. Donald Bliss, an insurance agent from the Detroit area, for $26,000 in 1958.

In 1961, it was sold again to Bill Frabotta, a Detroit photographer and artist, who used the fog station as a summer cottage.

In 1992, Frabotta began a comprehensive three-year rebuilding and restoration project, and, along with his wife, Mary, converted the entire building into a premier bed-and-breakfast facility, with Mary playing the 106-year-old parlour grand piano for guests in the evenings.

It was selected by *American Historic Inns* as one of the ten most romantic of its kind in America, and rated in the top 15 establishments for providing the best gourmet breakfasts by *Bed and Breakfast* journal.

Spectacle Reef Light

Lake Huron, MI
Built: 1874
Style: Conical tower on concrete pier
No: 11730
Position: 45 46 24 N. 84 08 12 W
Focal plane: 86ft (26m)
Range: 17 miles (27km)

Spectacle Reef Light is located 11 miles (18km) east of the Straits of Mackinac, at the northern end of Lake Huron, Michigan.

The period between 1852 and the beginning of the 20th century saw great activity by the US Lighthouse Board on the Great Lakes, with 26 new lighthouses built Between 1852 and 1860 alone. Spectacle Reef was designed and built by Colonel Orlando M. Poe and Major Godfrey Weitzel, and was the most expensive lighthouse ever to be built on the Great Lakes. It is also reputed to be the most spectacular engineering achievement in lighthouse construction on Lake Huron, and ranks high among all the lighthouses on the Great Lakes.

The fact that two schooners had been wrecked on Spectacle Reef led Congress to agree to a lighthouse being built to mark this Lake Huron danger spot. Work commenced in 1870, but because of the severe winters, the $406,000 programme took 200 men four years to complete. During the particularly severe winter of 1873–74, the builders returned to the lighthouse to find it encased in a 30ft (9m) high iceberg and had to tunnel their way in.

The 86-ft tower was designed and constructed by General Sherman's chief engineer, O.M. Poe, being fabricated from solid stone for the first 34ft (10m). Equipped with two second-order Fresnel lenses, the light has a range of 17 miles.

St. Joseph North Pier Lights

St. Joseph, MI
Built: 1832 and 1907
Style: Cylindrical and octagonal towers
No: 19515
Position: 42 07 00 N. 86 29 42 W
Focal plane: 31ft (9.5m)
Range: 15 miles (24km)
Height: 30ft (9m)

No: 19520 (North Pier Inner Light)
Focal plane: 53ft (16m)
Range: 16 miles (26km)
Height: 53ft (16m)

A lighthouse built on the mainland in 1832 once served St. Joseph's harbour. This was superseded in 1907 by the St. Joseph North Pier Lights, to which mariners must keep in perpendicular alignment to stay in the safe channel when approaching the harbour entrance.

The outer range light is a cylindrical white tower housing a fifth-order Fresnel lens, while the inner light is a white octagonal tower equipped with a fourth-order lens.

Sturgeon Point Light

Alcona, MI
Built: 1870
Style: Conical tower attached to dwelling
No: 11345
Position: 44 42 42 N. 83 16 18 W
Focal plane: 69ft (21m)
Range: 14 miles (22.5km)
Height: 68ft (21m)

The Sturgeon Point Light is located on Lake Huron in Haynes Township, Alcona County, in north-eastern lower Michigan.

The presence of this lighthouse has unquestionably forestalled countless accidents. The Sturgeon Point Light guards a treacherous reef on Lake Huron, where several ships have been wrecked: these include the wooden steamer, *Marine City*, which burned out in 1880, the 233-ton schooner, *Venus*, which ran onto the rocks in 1887, and the *Ispeming*, which suffered the same fate in 1903.

The tower, built in 1870, houses a three-and-a-half-order Fresnel lens, which was automated in 1939.

In 1915, the light station became part of the US Coast Guard, and in 1939 the US Lighthouse Service also merged under the control of the US Coast Guard. By the 1940s, the light had become fully automated, and the Coast Guard withdrew all personnel in 1941, thereafter dismantling the life-saving station.

The life-saving bell was purloined in 1951, and was 'anonymously returned' in 2002 to the custody of the Alcona County Historical Society.

The tower is regularly open for climbing by the public (for a small fee to cover insurance costs) during the summer months, and there is also a museum that deserves a visit.

Tawas Point Light

Tawas City, MI
Built: 1853 and 1876
Style: Cylindrical

Originally known as Ottawa Point, the name was officially changed to Tawas Point in 1902. The Tawas Point Light is located in the Tawas Point State Park off Tawas Bay in Lake Huron in Baldwin Township in northern Michigan. The lighthouse marks the northern side of Saginaw Bay.

In 1850, Congress appropriated $5,000 for the construction of a lighthouse. In 1852, building commenced, and the lighthouse was commissioned in 1853.

Following the completion of the lighthouse, however, many problems were revealed, and shifting sands had led to the point being extended by nearly a mile. The structure was failing, moreover, and a shipping disaster in the 1870s led to the decision to construct a new lighthouse in 1875. In 1876, construction was completed, with a final cost of $30,000.

Tawas Point has been remodelled by the Michigan Department of Natural Resources, with the assistance and contributions from the Friends of Tawas Point State Park. The downstairs is a museum of lighthouse paraphernalia, while the upstairs is a mini-cabin available to the public for rent. The house itself is available for a one- or two-week stay for a fee, and with an agreement to act as a trained volunteer keeper.

The original light had been a fifth-order Fresnel lens, but this was upgraded when the building was replaced in 1876. It is one of only 70 such lenses that remain operational in the United States, 16 of which are in use on the Great Lakes, eight of which are in Michigan.

Waugoshance Light

Mackinaw City, MI
Built: 1851
Style: Conical crib
Position: 45 47 10.2 N. 85 5 28.2 W

Located in Emmet County, Michigan, the 76-ft (23-m) lighthouse was built over the Waugoshance Shoals, a dangerous hazard in the Straits of Mackinac. The area around Waugoshance Point is not only shallow, but it is also a large (in area) projection from the bottom of the lake.

The lighthouse, which had a fifth-order Fresnel lens, was decommissioned in 1912, when it was replaced by the White Shoal Light. The conical brick tower, standing on its crib, has lain abandoned ever since, perhaps because it is said to be haunted by the ghost of John Herman, a keeper who fell to his death from the parapet in 1894. The Waugoshance Lighthouse Preservation Society has since been established to renovate the lighthouse.

White River Light

Whitehall, MI
Built: 1875
Construction: Brick, Gothic style
Style: Octagonal
Range: 14 miles (23km)

The White River Light is located on Lake Michigan near the city of Whitehall, Michigan. It sits on a narrow peninsula of land separating Lake Michigan from White Lake.

This was an area of sawmills, attracting shipping to the region, and with a growing frequency of wrecks, the Michigan legislature officially approached Congress requesting a lighthouse at the entrance to White Lake on 19 Jan 1853.

While the lighthouse was undeniably necessary, for obvious reasons, the lumber barons and merchants of White Lake felt that the creation of a new channel from White Lake into Lake Michigan was of even more importance. Thus they too began lobbying to commence such an undertaking as quickly as possible. A channel was cut from Lake Michigan to the lake in 1870 and the lighthouse was built on the southern shore. The building was commissioned in 1875 and fitted with a third-order Fresnel lens. The station was decommissioned in 1966.

Some of the buildings still in existence consist of the tower and attached dwelling, the South Pier-Head Beacon light, oil house, woodshed or storage building and the privy.

The lighthouse is open to the public as a museum with regular hours posted from Memorial Weekend through 31 August. It is also open throughout September and October but with reduced hours. The museum has a number of artifacts taken from the passenger and freight shipping on the lakes, in addition to interesting information pertaining to the lighthouse itself.

White Shoal Light

Mackinaw City, MI
Built: 1910
Style: Conical tower on conical crib
No: 17750
Position: 45 50 30 N. 85 08 06 W
Focal plane: 125ft (38m)
Range: 17 miles (27km)

The White Shoal Light is located 20 miles (32km) west of the Mackinac Bridge in Lake Michigan. It is an active aid to navigation.

This crib-style lighthouse was built in 1910, at a cost of $225,000, to mark the western approaches to the Straits of Mackinac on Lake Michigan. The steel tower, which is painted with spiralling red-and-white stripes, originally held a second-order Fresnel lens. This was replaced with a 190-mm optic when the tower was automated.

In addition to a fog signal, the lighthouse also had a submersible bell that would toll the number '23' to warn off mariners. This early 20th-century technological innovation was an audible precursor to a mid-century innovation using radar, RACON, which was later installed at this location.

Because of growing freighter traffic in and through the Straits of Mackinac, this light was part of a larger plan to build more lighthouses to protect ships and mariners in the area.

CHAPTER FOUR

LIGHTHOUSES OF THE SOUTH-EAST

Amelia Island Light

Old Fernandina Beach, FL
Built: 1839
Style: Conical tower
No: 565
Position: 30 40 24 N. 81 26 30 W
Focal plane: 107ft (33m)
Range: W 23 miles/37km, R 19 miles/31km
Height: 64ft (19.5m)

The Amelia Island Light is located at the northern end of Amelia Island at the mouth of the St. Mary's river. It marks the entrance to Nassau Sound and Fernandina Beach's harbour in Florida.

The lighthouse stood for 18 years on Little Cumberland Island, Georgia, before it was dismantled and transported to the mouth of the St. Mary's river in 1839. The tower was extensively renovated in 1885, when it was equipped with its third-order Fresnel lens. The lighthouse station remains an active US Coast Guard base.

Ownership of the lighthouse was transferred from the United States Coast Guard to the City of Fernandina Beach in 2001. It sits among private property and can only be viewed from a distance.

Anclote Key Light

Anclote Island, FL
Built: 1887
Style: Skeletal
Height: 110ft (34m)

The Anclote Key Light is located at the mouth of the Anclote river, near Tarpon Springs, Florida, the lighthouse having been built in 1887 on what is the largest of the Anclote Keys.

Originally a relatively minor coastal lighthouse, when it was built, the Anclote Key Light gained in importance, around 20 years later when Tarpon Springs became the world's leading producer of sponges. After harvesting sponges from the bottom of the Gulf of Mexico, the divers in their vessels used the light as a guide into the Anclote river and on to the Tarpon Springs Sponge Exchange.

This is reputed to be the sixth oldest standing lighthouse that was built using skeletal, tubular, cast-iron construction. Towers of this type were built in a number of locations where shifting sand or mud meant that the lighthouse might have to be moved, as was the case with the Cape San Blas Light in 1919. The open skeletal framework also allowed hurricane-force winds to pass right through the structure.

After the lighthouse was automated in 1952, the tower and other buildings on the site were often vandalized, interfering with the operation of the light. The Coast Guard determined that the light was no longer needed and it was deactivated in 1984.

The site was eventually turned over to the state of Florida and added to the Anclote Key Preserve State Park. By 2003, the lighthouse had been restored and relit using a reproduction fourth-order Fresnel lens. Anclote Key is accessible only by boat.

Assateague Island Light

Assateague, VA
Built: 1833 and 1867
Style: Conical tower
No: 275
Position: 37 54 40 N. 75 21 22 W
Focal plane: 154ft (47m)
Range: 22 miles (35km)
Height: 142ft (43m)

The Assateague Island Light is located at the southern end of Assateague Island off the coast of the Virginia Eastern Shore. It is sited within the Chincoteague National Wildlife Refuge and can be accessed by road from Chincoteague Island over the Assateague Channel.

Assateague, as a barrier island, is constantly changing, and southward growth has left the light stranded 5 miles (8km) from Chincoteague Inlet. As an eastern seaboard lighthouse, however, Assateague's striking red-and-white striping makes it a distinctive day marker. The lighthouse is managed by the US Coast Guard and is still in use today.

The first lighthouse, built on top of a 22-ft (7-m) bluff, was a 45-ft (14-m) stone tower completed in 1833. But it was neither high enough nor bright enough to prevent vessels from running up on the hazardous shoals that extended from the island. The light was eventually replaced with the present red-and-white-banded conical brick tower in 1867. It was equipped with a first-order Fresnel lens, but an aero-marine beacon replaced this when the station was automated in 1967.

The Assateague Light is approximately a quarter of a mile away from Chincoteague Island and visitors can drive there from Chincoteague in about five minutes. Some people elect to rent bicycles or walk along the trail that leads from Chincoteague over to Assateague Island.

Bald Head (Cape Fear) Light

Bald Head Island, Southport, NC
Built: 1794 and 1818
Style: Octagonal

The Bald Head Light, nicknamed Old Baldy, is the oldest lighthouse still standing in North Carolina. It is the second of three lighthouses that have been built on Bald Head Island since the 18th century to help guide ships past the dangerous shoals at the mouth of the Cape Fear river.

The present 110-ft (33.5-m) lighthouse has marked the entrance to the river since 1818. The brick-built tower replaced an earlier lighthouse, erected in 1794, which was soon threatened by severe erosion of the river bank. Consequently, the existing tower was built with walls 5-ft (1.5-m) thick at the base. The station's light was originally powered by a series of whale-oil lamps, which were later replaced by a fourth-order Fresnel lens. The tower was decommissioned in 1935.

The Old Baldy Foundation operates Old Baldy and the adjacent Smith Island Museum of History, which is located in a replica of one of the original keeper's quarters from the 1850s, and features period furnishings, lighthouse artifacts (including parts of the lens from the Cape Fear Light), and exhibits illustrating the history of Old Baldy and the island.

Requests for funds to raise the height of Old Baldy and install a more powerful first-order lens to make it a coastal beacon were never approved. Instead, in 1898, the Lighthouse Board agreed to the construction of a new 159-ft (48-m) steel skeleton tower equipped with a first-order lens named the Cape Fear Light, to be located on the south-eastern end of Bald Head Island, where it would mark the shoals. It served as a coastal beacon from 1903 to 1958.

Biloxi Light

Biloxi, MS
Built: 1848
Style: Conical tower
No: 7785
Position: 30 23 42 N. 88 54 06 W
Focal plane: 61ft (18.5m)

The Biloxi Light, in Biloxi, Mississippi, is sited adjacent to the Mississippi Sound of the Gulf of Mexico. Biloxi now stands like a traffic signal on the central reservation of US Highway 90, which bisects the narrow peninsula on which Biloxi stands. The tower's fifth-order Fresnel lens was buried for protection during the Civil War and the brick-lined, cast-iron structure has withstood many assaults, including Hurricane Camille, which destroyed the keeper's quarters in 1968.

The lighthouse has had female keepers for more years than any other lighthouse in the United States, having been manned by females for 81 years of its working life. Maria Younghans, who tended the light for 51 years, was the first female keeper in the history of the service, and her daughter, Miranda, succeeded her.

The lighthouse, which was automated in 1926, is now maintained by the city of Biloxi as a private aid to navigation.

Today, it is no longer just a beacon to seafarers, but a tangible testament of resilience. The Biloxi Light, erected in 1848 and one of the first cast-iron lighthouses in the south, is the city's signature landmark and has become a post-Katrina symbol of the city's resolve, representing all who have ever weathered a storm.

In March 2010, the city re-opened the lighthouse to public tours after a 14-month, $400,000 restoration, that was completed by Biloxi contractor J.O. Collins.

Cape Canaveral Light

Cape Canaveral, FL
Built: 1848 and 1868
No: 625
Position: 28 27 37 N. 80 32 36 W
Focal plane: 137ft (42m)
Range: 24 miles (39km)
Height: 145ft (44m)

Cape Canaveral, as it was formerly known, is now best-known for the Kennedy Space Center, but in the 19th century it was the treacherous shoals surrounding the cape that marked it out for special attention.

A 65-ft (20-m) brick lighthouse was erected in 1848 to counter the problem, but its feeble light did more harm than good, for crews often ran their ships aground looking for the signal. After the Civil War, the tower was replaced with the current 145-ft brick-lined, cast-iron lighthouse. Finished in 1868, it had a giant 'clamshell' first-order Fresnel lens and a range of 18 miles. In 1893, sea erosion led to the lighthouse being moved a mile inland. The tower's Fresnel lens was replaced with an aero-marine beacon when the station was automated in 1993, and the original lantern is now on display at the Ponce Inlet Museum.

In 2003, the oil house was restored to its original (1890s) state (strong winds had damaged the roof in the 1970s and a window was added in the early 1900s). In 2006, another project restored the lantern room and the structure was repainted using modern materials.

The Cape Canaveral Lighthouse Foundation and volunteers are instrumental in restoration projects and in interpreting the lighthouse's history. The lighthouse, however, is hardly the main attraction, and the bus tour that passes by it also includes stops at the original Mercury and Gemini launch pads and Mission Control Centers.

Cape Florida Light

Key Biscayne, FL
Built: 1825
Style: Conical
Position: 25 39 59 72 N. 80 9 21.47 W
Height: 95ft (29m)

The Cape Florida Light is located on Cape Florida at the southern end of Key Biscayne in Miami-Dade County, Florida.

The original 65-ft (20-m) lighthouse faced an unusual threat when it was attacked by a Seminole war party in 1836. Unable to flush out the keeper and his assistant, the warriors set fire to the tower. The assistant keeper was killed, but John Thompson, the keeper, who was badly burned, survived the attack by clinging to a ledge at the top of the tower until the arrival of a naval warship saved his life.

The tower survived, but because of the threat of further attacks, stood empty for ten years. When it was brought back into operation in 1846, its height was raised to 95ft. The station was decommissioned in 1878, replaced by the Fowey Rocks Light.

In 1898, in response to the growing tension with Spain over Cuba that resulted in the Spanish-American War, the Cape Florida Light briefly became US Signal Station Number Four, one of 36 such stations along the east coast and Gulf Coast from Maine to Texas.

The southern third of Key Biscayne, including the lighthouse, was bought by the state of Florida in 1966, and became what is now the Bill Baggs Cape Florida State Park. The lighthouse tower and keeper's house have been restored. In 1978 the US Coast Guard installed an automated light in the tower as a navigational aid, particularly to help boaters find the Florida Channel at night. It was relit during the 1996 Miami Centennial celebrations.

Cape Hatteras Light

Cape Hatteras, NC
Built: 1803, 1870 and 1999
Style: Tower with brick base
No: 625
Position: 35 15 08 N. 75 31 44 W
Focal plane: 192ft (58.5m)
Range: 24 miles (39km)

With its lofty, spirally-banded black-and-white tower, the 191-ft (58-m) Cape Hatteras Light is one of the world's best-known maritime sentinels, being easily spotted not only by ships but also by orbiting spacecraft!

It overlooks Cape Hatteras, where the warm waters of the Gulf Stream meet the colder Labrador Current, and warns ships of the dangerous Diamond Shoals offshore.

The earlier 95-ft (29-m) sentinel of 1803 was condemned as totally inadequate by naval inspectors, and the present tower replaced it after the Civil War. By the 1990s it was threatened by coastal erosion, and in 1999 the tower was moved on tracks in a $12-million operation to save this American icon from falling into the sea.

When the tower was abandoned for a period during the 1930s, souvenir hunters took the prismatic elements of the first-order Fresnel lens as mementos, and it is now equipped with an aero-marine beacon.

For a number of years, climbing to the top was not possible due to repairs being made to the lighthouse, but the National Park Service now permits visitors to do so; the climb, however, is considered strenuous because it is equivalent to 12 storeys. There is a handrail only on one side of the stairs, and no two-way traffic on them is possible. The lighthouse is open for tours from the third Friday in April to Columbus Day.

Cape Lookout Light

Beaufort, NC
Built: 1812 and 1859
Style: Black-and-white tower
No: 670
Position: 34 37 22 N. 76 31 28 W
Focal plane: 156ft (47.5m)
Range: 25 miles (40km)

The present Cape Lookout Light was built in 1859 on Core Banks Island. It is the second lighthouse that has stood at this location, and it is nearly identical to the Bodie Island Light, which has horizontal stripes.

The first Cape Lookout Light was completed and lit in 1812 at a cost of more than $20,000, which Congress authorized in 1804. It was the fourth lighthouse to be built in North Carolina and was a 96-ft (29-m) brick tower with wooden shingles painted with red-and-white horizontal stripes. But it proved to be too short to light the treacherous Lookout Shoals, which were nicknamed the 'Horrible Headland'.

The existing tower was fitted with a third-order Fresnel lens, but this was shot at by Confederate troops retreating from Fort Macon during the Civil War. A first-order Fresnel lens replaced it in 1864 when hostilities had ceased. That in turn has since been replaced by an aero-marine beacon, which gives the tower a range of 25 miles.

The lighthouse is part of the Cape Lookout National Seashore and can only be accessed by private ferry. A few times a year, visitors are allowed to climb the 201 spiral iron steps to the top of the lighthouse. During the summer, the Cape Lookout Light Station Visitor Center and Keepers' Quarters are also open to the public. Though tower climbs were suspended in February 2008, the lighthouse opened for climbing permanently on 15 July 2010.

Cape San Blas Light

Apalachicola, FL
Built: 1847, 1856, 1859 and 1885
Style: Skeletal tower
Position: 29 40 16.41 N. 85 21 22.72 W
Range: 16 miles (26km)
Height: 98ft (30m)

Cape San Blas Light is located south-west of Port St. Joe, Florida.

There has been a light to warn ships of the dangerous shoals around Cape San Blas since 1847, but hurricanes, coupled with a constantly eroding coastline, has led to the lighthouse being replaced three times.

The first tower stood for just four years before a hurricane knocked it down in 1851. Yellow fever delayed the construction of a new tower for four years, but this too was toppled by a hurricane almost immediately.

The third tower was destroyed during a Confederate raid in 1859 and, though rebuilt after the Civil War, the fourth tower stood only until 1882 when erosion led to it collapsing into the sea.

This sorry saga continued when the ship carrying the materials for the tower's replacement struck a shoal off Sanibel Island and sank. When the new tower was finally built in 1885, a steel skeleton structure was adopted with the intention that when erosion threatened again it could be dismantled and moved farther inland. Ironically, this tower, which was equipped with a third-order flashing Fresnel lens, has stood the test of time ever since, although progress in other navigational aids led to its light being decommissioned in 1991.

The lighthouse is now a white, square skeleton tower, enclosing a stair cylinder, with the lantern 98ft above ground and 101ft above water. A radiobeacon was established at the station in 1939.

Cape St. George Light

St. George Island, FL
Built: 1833 and 1852
Style: Conical

The original 70-ft (21-m) St. George Island Light was built by Winslow Lewis in 1833 to guide cotton freighters into the bay, but was so inadequate that its light was only visible a few miles out to sea. The tower was destroyed in 1851 by the same hurricane that toppled a number of other lighthouses across Florida, including the Cape San Blas Light.

The station was rebuilt in 1852 and since then the 74-ft (22.5-m) tower has stood up to dozens of major storms, as well as a cannonade from Confederates during the Civil War. Instead, beach erosion has proved to be its Achilles heel. The light's third-order Fresnel lens was deactivated in 1994.

In 1995 Hurricane Opal washed away much of the sand around the tower, shifted the tower partially off its pilings and rotated it, leaving it leaning about 10° from the vertical. In 1998 the tower was further damaged by Hurricane Georges, following which supporters raised $50,000 locally and $160,000 from the state to correct the tilt. The tower was righted and a new foundation was built under it in 2002. The base, however, was still exposed to surf, and the new foundation began to deteriorate. The tower eventually collapsed on 22 October 2005.

Island volunteers formed the St. George Light Association to reconstruct the lighthouse on a more protected site. A salvage company retrieved 24,000 of the structure's 160,000 bricks from the water, and volunteers cleaned them up. The salvaged bricks were used in the interior lining of the conical tower.

The association won grants of $525,000 from federal and state sources, and rebuilt the lighthouse in a county park in the middle of St. George Island, with local contractors providing construction services at reduced rates. In April 2008, the restored lantern room was placed on top. The completed reconstruction was opened to the public on 29 November.

Chesapeake Lightship

Built: 1930
Builder: Charleston Dry Dock & Machine
 Co., SC
No: 116
Length overall: 133ft 3in (41m)
Beam: 30ft (9m)
Draft: 13ft (4m)

Illuminating apparatus: One 375-mm electric
lens lantern at each masthead

Design: Diesel-electric-propelled; steel hull;
 two masts; smokestack amidships

The lightship *Chesapeake* was caught in the
path of a hurricane in 1936, but amazingly
survived with very little damage. She served
in the Chesapeake Bay area for 40 years
and, having been decommissioned in 1970,
was placed on public display at Hams Point
in Washington, DC, and subsequently in
Baltimore's inner harbour.

Station Assignments
1930–33: Fenwick Island Shoal (DE)
1933–42: Chesapeake Bay (VA)
1942–45: Examination vessel (wartime)
1945–65: Chesapeake Bay (VA)
1965–70: Delaware (DE)
1971–80: Displayed at Hams Point,
 Washington, D.C.
1982: Baltimore Harbor Place,
 Constellation Dock

Cockspur Island Light

Savannah, GA
Built: 1849
Style: Conical

The Cockspur Island Light is a small lighthouse located in Chatham County, Georgia.

The 36-ft (11-m) lighthouse is the sole survivor of a pair of lights built in 1849 to mark the north and south channels of the Savannah river. The tower survived the crossfire that destroyed its twin during the Civil War, but is now increasingly threatened by rising waters.

The lighthouse is built on an oyster and mussel bed. It is unique in that the base is shaped like the bow of a ship to reduce the impact of the waves on the structure. The tower, which held a fourth-order Fresnel lens, was decommissioned in 1949.

Starting in 1995 and lasting until 2000, the upper portions of the lighthouse were restored, although the foundations still require protection from wave action and tidal erosion.

On 18 March 2007, at 7:30pm, the lighthouse was relit in a ceremony hosted by the National Park Service and the US Coast Guard for historical rather than navigational purposes.

The lighthouse is open to the public although no official tours or accommodations are made. However, visitors to the area frequently access the beacon by kayak.

The National Park Service bushwacked a trail to the lighthouse in 2005 to allow visitors a closer vantage point. The trail begins on the north-eastern side of the fort and is more than three-quarters of a mile long. At low tide, this has enabled hikers to get within approximately 200 yards of the lighthouse.

Concord Point Light

Havre de Grace, MD
Position: 39 32 26.52 N. 76 55.28 W
Built: 1827
Style: Conical
Height: 32ft (10m)

Concord Point is a lighthouse in Havre de Grace, Maryland, overlooking the point where the Susquehanna river flows into the Chesapeake Bay, an area of increasing navigational traffic at the time it was constructed in 1827. It is the most northerly lighthouse in Maryland and the oldest continuously-operated lighthouse in the state.

To protect ships from the dangerous shoals and currents at the mouth of the Susquehanna river, the town of Havre de Grace deeded the US Government a 484-ft² piece of land in 1826 for the purpose of establishing a lighthouse. John Donahoo was hired to do the construction, and on 21 May 1827 the completed lighthouse was commissioned.

The 32-ft stone lighthouse was built at a cost of $3,500, placing the light at a height above seawater of 38.5ft (12m). Designed as a conical stone tower, the walls were constructed of granite that were nearly 4ft (1.2m) thick at the base and 18in (46cm) thick at the top. The tower was originally fitted with an array of lamps and 16-in (406-mm) reflectors, but now uses a fifth-order Fresnel lens.

In 1812 John O'Neil staged a successful one-man stand against a squadron of British warships and, as a reward, was nominated keeper of the lighthouse. The job passed down the generations until the tower was automated in the 1920s. The light is now maintained as a private aid to navigation.

The lighthouse is maintained by The Friends of Concord Point Lighthouse.

Currituck Beach Light

Corolla, NC
Built: 1874
Style: Conical tower
No: 555
Position: 36 22 37 N. 75 49 47 W
Focal plane: 158ft (48m)
Range: 18 miles (29km)
Height: 163ft (50m)

The Currituck Beach Light is located on the Outer Banks in Corolla, North Carolina.

The brick-built lighthouse was erected in 1874 as part of a chain of lights along the Carolina Outer Banks, It alerted vessels, that elected to take an inshore course to avoid the adverse flow of the Gulf Stream, to the proximity of the shoals and sandbanks that have sunk so many ships in the past. The red tower, which has walls 6-ft (2-m) thick at the base, still has its original 12-ft (4-m) first-order Fresnel bull's-eye lens, giving the beam a range of 18 miles.

The Outer Banks Conservationists (OBC) have performed much of the reconstruction and refurbishing work since 1980 through private funding and volunteer work. Since 1991, visitors have been allowed to climb the original 214 steps to the outdoor gallery. Access to the lens room is not permitted as the first-order lens is not only the original, but is also still a functioning one. The light comes on every night, flashing at 20-second intervals to warn ships hugging the chain of barrier islands along the coast.

In 2003 the federal government granted OBC title to the lighthouse itself, the Coast Guard having approved OBC's ownership proposal over that of an application submitted by Currituck County (the county in which the lighthouse is located). OBC remains the owner of the Currituck Beach Lighthouse.

Drum Point Light

Solomons, MD
Built: 1883
Style: Hexagonal screwpile
Position: 38 19 51.6 N. 76 27 46.8 W

The lighthouse was built in 1883, at a cost of $5,000, to mark a sandy spit that threatened vessels passing Drum Point on the northern side of the entrance to the Patuxent river. A fourth-order Fresnel lens served the lighthouse until it was decommissioned in 1962.

The light had been needed in the first place because of the considerable shoaling around the point. This gradually shifted the shoreline to the point where the light, which originally stood in 10ft of water, was entirely on land by 1970. When vandalism and neglect threatened its future in 1975, the tower was moved in one piece to the Calvert Marine Museum, where it now stands.

Restoration was aided by many grants and the donation of period furnishings, and the light was rededicated as an exhibit in June 1978. Fortuitously, the complete logbooks from 1883 to 1943 also survive.

Dry Tortugas Light

Loggerhead Key, Dry Tortugas, FL
Built: 1858
Style: Conical tower
No: 1095
Position: 24 38 00 N. 82 55 12 W
Focal plane: 151ft (46m)
Range: 20 miles (32km)
Height: 151ft (46m)

The Dry Tortugas Light is located on Loggerhead Key, three miles west of Fort Jefferson, Florida.

The lower half of the lighthouse is white, the upper half black, and it was built to supplement the weak light at Garden Key.

Built for $35,000, its height, coupled with a second-order Fresnel lens, gave the beacon a range of 20 miles, which was more than enough to keep passing ships away from the shoals.

The tower was severely damaged in 1873 by the same hurricane that destroyed Garden Key Light, but the repair work was so effective that the tower still stands today. The station was automated in 1925, and its original 'clamshell' Fresnel lens was replaced by a modern optic in 1986.

Egmont Key Light

St. Petersburg, FL
Built: 1848 and 1858
Style: White tower
No: 1370
Position: 27 36 03 N. 82 45 38 W
Focal plane: 85ft (26m)

Range: 24 miles (39km)
Height 87ft (26.5m)

The Egmont Key Light, on the Gulf Coast, was the first of several towers built by Francis Gibbons to serve the Tampa Bay region. The original tower was built in 1848 but was destroyed ten years later by a hurricane. The present 87-ft white masonry tower that replaced it has walls 3ft (1m) thick to prevent this from happening again. The original first-order Fresnel lens was replaced by an aero-marine beacon when the station was automated.

Fowey Rocks Light

Cape Florida, FL
Built:1878
Style: Octagonal pyramidal skeleton tower
No: 920
Position: 25 35 24 N. 80 05 48 W
Focal plane: 110ft (33.5m)
Range: W 15 miles/24km, R 10 miles/16km
Height 110ft (33.5m)

Fowey Rocks Light is located seven miles south-east of Cape Florida on Key Biscayne. The lighthouse was completed in 1878, replacing the Cape Florida Light. It was automated on 7 May 1974 and is still in operation today.

The structure is made of cast iron, with a screwpile foundation, a platform and a skeletal tower. The light stands 110ft above the water. The tower framework is painted brown, while the dwelling and enclosed circular stair to the lantern is painted white.

The original lens was a first-order drum Fresnel lens which stood about 12ft (4m) high and weighed about a ton. The light has a nominal range of 15 miles in the white sectors, and 10 miles in the red sectors.

Fowey Rocks are named for the Royal Navy frigate, HMS *Fowey*, which was wrecked on a different reef to the south in 1748. During construction of the lighthouse the workers lived on a platform built over the water to minimize the danger of transporting them and their supplies each day from the mainland.

The Labor Day Hurricane of 1935 washed away the first deck of the lighthouse, which was 15ft above the water, but the tower survived. The lighthouse is located inside the boundaries of Biscayne National Park. In June 2011, the light (along with 11 others) was made available at no cost to public organizations willing to preserve them.

Garden Key Light

Fort Jefferson, Dry Tortugas, FL
Built: 1826 and 1876
Style: Conical
Position 24 37 41 N. 82 52 20 W
Height: 70ft (21m)

The Garden Key Light, also known as the Tortuga Harbor Light, is located at Fort Jefferson, on Garden Key in the Dry Tortugas, Florida.

The original 70-ft brick lighthouse at Garden Key was one of Florida's earliest light stations. Built in 1826, the lighthouse warned mariners of the reefs and low-lying islands that make up the Dry Tortugas archipelago. The need for a light here was reinforced when the ship, carrying the building materials, was wrecked on the very shoals the lighthouse was intended to guard.

A few years after its construction, the tower gained a new neighbour in the form of Fort Jefferson, which was built to protect the vital sea lanes linking the Caribbean and the Atlantic with the Gulf of Mexico.

By 1846 the fort had grown so large that the Garden Key Light was barely visible above the ramparts, so when the tower was severely damaged by a hurricane in 1873, its 37-ft (11-m) cast-iron replacement was built on top of the fort. The lighthouse was equipped with a fourth-order Fresnel lens giving the light a range of 16 miles (26km). The tower remains, but the light was deactivated in 1924.

Ernest Hemingway's 1932 short story, *After the Storm*, is about a shipwreck that occurred between Garden Key and Rebecca Shoal, to the east of Garden Key.

Georgetown Light

Georgetown, SC
Built: 1801 and 1812
Style: Cylindrical tower
No: 120
Position: 33 13 24 N. 79 11 06 W
Focal plane: 85ft (26m)
Range: 15 miles (24km)

The Georgetown Light is situated on North Island at the entrance to Winyah Bay, south-east of Georgetown.

The present 87-ft (26.5-m) lighthouse, built in 1812, is the oldest active tower in South Carolina. It replaced an earlier 72-ft (22-m) wooden tower, which was blown down during a cyclone in 1806. The present white brick tower was badly damaged during the Civil War, but was renovated in 1867 and has continued ever since. The light was automated in 1986 when its original Fresnel lens was replaced by a solar-powered optic.

The light is maintained by the US Coast Guard, and the lighthouse is now under the control of the state of South Carolina as part of the Tom Yawkey Wildlife Center Heritage Preserve.

Harbor Town Light

Harbor Town, Hilton Head Island, SC
Built: 1970
Style: Octagonal
Position: 32 8 19 N. 80 48 46 W
Height 90ft (27m)

The Harbor Town Light can be seen at the Harbor Town Marina, on Hilton Head Island. The lighthouse was privately built and is a private aid to navigation.

Although initially ridiculed during the planning and construction phases, the lighthouse became instantly popular and is today the most recognizable symbol of Hilton Head Island and the Sea Pines Resort. The annually televised *The Heritage* golf tournament has helped to increase the lighthouse's fame to millions of golf fans worldwide, and the 18th hole, at the Harbor Town Golf Links, has become one of the most popular and recognizable of the finishing holes in golf.

The construction of the Harbor Town Light was begun in 1969 by Charles Fraser, and was completed in 1970. It takes the form of a hexagonal column with a red observation deck or gallery below the lantern. The column is stucco on metal lath over plywood, with a height of 90ft. The lighthouse's daymark consists of alternating red-and-white bands. It has a white light that flashes every 2.5 seconds.

The lighthouse was privately built as part of the Harbor Town Marina and Sea Pines Plantation, being an aid to navigation to guide vessels between the Inland Waterway and Calibogue Sound. It is open for the public to climb, but there is a small fee for a day pass to the plantation and another for admission to its lighthouse.

Hillsboro Inlet Light

Pompano Beach, FL
Built: 1907
Style: Octagonal iron skeleton tower
No: 775
Position: 26 15 33 N. 80 04 51 W
Focal plane: 136ft (41.5m)
Range: 28 miles (45km)
Height: 136ft (41.5m)

Hillsboro Inlet Light is located on the north side of Hillsboro Inlet, midway between Fort Lauderdale and Boca Raton. The light marks the northern limit of the Florida Reef, an underwater coral formation on the lower east coast of the state of Florida.

In 1901, the United States Lighthouse Establishment persuaded Congress to authorize the construction of a lighthouse in the dark area between the Jupiter Inlet Light and the Fowey Rocks Light. Hillsboro Inlet Light is considered to be one of the most powerful lights in the world, with a beam that can be seen for 28 miles.

The octagonal iron pyramidal tower was built at the Russel Wheel & Foundry Company in Detroit, Michigan, moved to Florida in 1906, and lit on 7 March 1907.

Its second-order bivalve Fresnel lens emits a light measuring 5.5 megacandelas and is sited 136ft above sea level. Automated in 1974, the light acts both as a coastal navigational aid and as a support to local water traffic.

In years past, this lighthouse has witnessed rum and drug smugglers, many hurricanes, and German submarines. Today, an armada of luxury yachts, sport-fishing boats, and private sailing craft are more usual visitors to this waterway.

The US Coast Guard operates the Hillsboro Inlet Light Light and it is not open to the public.

Hooper Island Light

Hoopersville, MD
Built: 1902
Style: White conical tower on cylinder
No: 7590
Position: 38 15 24 N. 76 15 00 W

Focal plane: 63ft (19m)
Range: 9 miles (14.5km)

The Hooper Island Light is located in Chesapeake Bay, west of Middle Hooper Island in Maryland.

The 35-ft (11-m) cast-iron, spark-plug-style lighthouse stands on a massive cast-iron and concrete caisson. It was the last lighthouse to be built in Chesapeake Bay and, though still in operation, its fourth-order Fresnel lens has been replaced by a modern optic.

149

Hunting Island Light

Beaufort, SC
Built: 1859, 1875 and 1889
Style: Conical
Position: 32 22 30 N. 80 26 18 W
Height: 136ft (41.5m)

The Hunting Island Light is located in Hunting Island State Park on Hunting Island near Beaufort. The first lighthouse, built in 1859, was lost during the Civil War. A 134-ft (41-m) brick-lined cast-iron replacement was built in 1875, but when erosion threatened the structure in 1889, the tower was dismantled and rebuilt a mile from the original site. The station was equipped with a second-order Fresnel lens until it was decommissioned in 1933. This is the only lighthouse in the state of South Carolina that is open to the public.

Jupiter Inlet Light

Jupiter, FL
Built: 1860
Style: Red brick tower
No: 725
Position: 26 56 55 N. 80 04 55 W
Focal plane: 146ft (44.5m)
Range: 25 miles (40km)
Height: 108ft (33m)

The Jupiter Inlet Light is located in Jupiter, Florida, on the northern side of the Jupiter Inlet, the site having been chosen in 1853. It lies between the Cape Canaveral and Hillsboro Inlet Lights.

The construction of the lighthouse, in 1860, was overseen by two army engineers, who later met on opposing sides at Gettysburg. The site was surveyed by Robert E. Lee, while George Meade was responsible for its construction.

The Civil War also affected the tower, for the light was extinguished by Confederate raiders a year after its completion. The tower remained dark until keeper, James Armour, found the tower's first-order Fresnel lens hidden in a creek a year later. This lens remains in use today. The tower has also taken its share of battering from the weather. In 1928, a hurricane knocked out both the primary and emergency electric power, which forced Charles Seabrook, the keeper, to resurrect the station's old mineral lamps. When the keeper became exhausted, his 16-year-old son took over the job of rotating the giant lens by hand and keeping the light burning.

The lighthouse was built on an Indian shell mound (midden). The top of the 108-ft tower is 146ft (45m) above sea level, the light having a range of 25 miles. The walls are 31in (79cm) thick at the base, tapering to 18in near the top. The tower was left unpainted for the first 50 years, but had grown so discoloured that it was painted red in around 1910.

Key West Light

Key West, FL
Built: 1825 and 1849
Style: Conical

The Key West Light is located in Key West, Florida. The first lighthouse was a 65-ft (20m) tower, which was completed in 1825 and had 15 lamps in 15-in (380-mm) reflectors. The great Havana hurricane of 1846 destroyed the lighthouse, the same hurricane also destroying the Sand Key Light, located eight miles (13km) away.

As both lighthouses serving Key West had now been destroyed, a ship was acquired and outfitted as a lightship to serve as the Sand Key Light until new lighthouses could be built. Due to efforts to reorganize the Lighthouse Board, Congress was slow to appropriate funds for the new lighthouses, but the new tower for the Key West Light was completed in 1849. It had 13 lamps in 21-in (533-mm) reflectors, and stood on ground about 15ft (4.6m) above sea level. In 1858 the light received a third-order Fresnel lens. In 1873 the lantern was replaced, having been damaged by a hurricane in 1866, which added 3ft to the height of the tower. The growth of trees and taller buildings in Key West began to obscure the light, and in 1894 the tower was raised 20ft, placing the light about 100ft (30m) above sea level.

After the US Coast Guard decommissioned the Key West Light in 1969, it was turned over to Monroe County, which in turn leased it to the Key West Arts and Historical Society. The society operates the lighthouse and its associated buildings as the Key West Light House and Keepers' Quarters Museum. On display at the museum is the first-order Fresnel lens from the Sombrero Key Light.

Klein Curaçao Light

Klein Curaçao, Curaçao
Built: 1879
Style: Cylindrical
No. J6400
Focal plane: 75ft (23m)
Range: 14 miles (22.5km)
Height: 75ft (23m)

Curaçao is an island in the southern Caribbean Sea, off the Venezuelan coast. The Country of Curaçao includes the main island plus the small, uninhabited island of Klein Curaçao ('Little Curaçao'), and is a constituent country of the Kingdom of the Netherlands.

The barren island of Klein Curaçao is located 7 miles (11km) off the south-eastern tip of Curaçao. Located at the centre of the island, the lighthouse is accessible only by boat.

The lighthouse was built in 1879 to warn vessels of the presence of this featureless, almost flat island. The lighthouse is the only permanent structure on the island, which is uninhabited other than by fishermen using it as a temporary base.

The white, cylindrical, coral-brick tower has an attached two-storey keeper's dwelling. The light is now automated, but there was an interim period when the lighthouse was lit and extinguished each day by a keeper, who accessed the island by boat. The beacon now runs on solar power, but the buildings themselves are in dire need of repair.

Morris Island Light

Charleston, SC
Built: 1767 and 1876
Style: Conical stone tower

The Morris Island Light is located on Morris Island in South Carolina. The lighthouse stands on the southern side of the entrance to Charleston harbour, north of the city of Folly Beach.

Marine erosion has played a significant role in the history and ultimately the demise of the Morris Island Light as an active aid to navigation. The first tower, built as long ago as 1767, was sidelined, first by the Civil War and then by the silting-up of the waterways around Charleston harbour.

The present 161-ft (49-m) black-and-white-striped tower was built on a concrete foundation 8ft (2.5m) thick, laid on wooden piles driven 50ft (15m) into the mud. Fitted with a first-order Fresnel lens, the tower was automated in 1938 and decommissioned in 1962. It was built well inland, but erosion has left the structure isolated on what is now Morris Island, several hundred feet from the shore.

In 1999, Save The Light, Incorporated purchased the historic lighthouse for $75,000 to preserve it for the people of South Carolina. In 2000, the lighthouse was transferred to the state of South Carolina and was then leased to Save The Light for 99 years to co-ordinate the stabilization, erosion control and restoration of the building, and to raise the necessary funds for the work. In 2007, Save The Light hosted a successful event, in which the lighthouse was lit up once again, but only for a day, and many people went to Morris Island by boat to witness the festivities. The Morris Island Light now has a cement barrier built around it, offering it protection in the years to come.

New & Old Cape Henry Lights

New Cape Henry Light

Virginia Beach, VA

Built: 1872 and 1881

Style: Octagonal covered with iron plates

Focal plane: 350ft (107m)

Range: W 17 miles/27km, R 15 miles/24km

Height: 163ft (50m)

The present lighthouse was built to mark the entrance to Chesapeake Bay, replacing the original lighthouse of 1872. The black-and-white masonry tower, which is protected by iron plates, is still equipped with its original first-order Fresnel lens.

Old Cape Henry Light

Virginia Beach, VA

Built: 1792

Style: Octagonal

The 90-ft (27-m) Old Cape Henry Light, which dates back to 1792, was one of the first building projects commissioned after the

War of Independence. The lighthouse, which marked the entrance to Chesapeake Bay, developed serious cracks in its stonework during the 1870s and was replaced by the New Cape Henry Light in 1881. The original tower, however, has defied nature for well over a century since then and is now a national monument.

Ocracoke Island Light

Ocracoke Island, NC
Built: 1818 and 1823
No: 660
Position: 35 06 32 N. 75 59 10 W

North Carolina's Outer Banks' island of Ocracoke has been no stranger to sea-faring history, in that Sir Walter Raleigh's expeditions touched land here in the late 1500s. Ocracoke's most famous son, however, was Edward Teach, otherwise known as Blackbeard the Pirate, who used the island as a hideout during his looting expeditions.

Ocracoke was also the place where Blackbeard died, beheaded, not without a struggle, by the British naval officer, Robert Maynard, in 1718. Some legends have it that Blackbeard's body swam around Maynard's vessel a few times after it had been decapitated, and there is still the belief that Blackbeard haunts the vicinity.

The Ocracoke Light is the oldest operating light station in North Carolina. It was built on Ocracoke Island, in Hyde County, by Noah Porter, a Massachusetts builder. In 1864, Confederate troops dismantled the fourth-order Fresnel lens, but Union forces later restored it.

The present 65-ft (20-m) lighthouse was built in 1823 to replace an earlier tower situated on Shell Castle Island, which was struck by lightning in 1818. The tower was equipped with a fourth-order Fresnel lens, which was replaced by a modern optic when the station was automated in 1955. The light has a range of 14 miles (22.5km).

During the summer months, when there is a US National Park ranger on duty, visitors may enter the base of the lighthouse, but climbing the tower for the view from the top is, unfortunately, not permitted.

Pensacola Light

Pensacola, FL
Built: 1824 and 1858
Style: Conical brick tower
No: 180
Position: 30 20 48 N. 87 18 30 W
Focal plane: 191ft (58m)
Range: 27 miles (43.5km)
Height: 171ft (52m)

The Pensacola Light is situated at the entrance to Pensacola Bay, at Pensacola, in Florida.

The first guardian of the bay was the lightship, *Aurora Borealis*, it having been moved to Pensacola in 1823 from its previous post at the mouth of the Mississippi river after a lighthouse had superseded it. Because of frequent rough seas, the lightship had to be anchored inside the bay entrance, behind Santa Rosa Island, and could not reliably be seen from ships outside of the bay.

The original 45-ft (14-m) Winslow Lewis-designed lighthouse was built in 1824 to guide warships in and out of the Pensacola naval base. When the United States acquired Florida from Spain in 1819, President James Monroe ordered the navy to flush out pirates operating in the Gulf of Mexico, and Pensacola proved to be the perfect place for a permanent base.

The original lighthouse did not last long. Like so many other Winslow Lewis lighthouses, it was considered to be inadequate and was replaced in 1858 by the present 171-ft brick tower. Now automated, the tower's original first-order Fresnel lens still sheds its light 27 miles out to sea and remains an active aid to navigation.

Maintenance and tour operations are currently conducted by the Pensacola Lighthouse Association.

Ponce de Leon Inlet Light

Ponce Inlet, FL
Built: 1835 and 1887
Style: Red brick conical tower
No: 610
Position: 29 04 48 N. 80 55 42 W
Focal plane: 159ft (48.5m)
Range: 17 miles (27km)
Height: 159ft (48.5m)

The first attempt to build a lighthouse at Ponce de Leon Inlet was made in 1835, but the tower collapsed during a storm before the light had even been lit, and half a century passed before another attempt was made.

The present 159-ft tower was built in 1887, with bricks shipped from Baltimore, and it was fitted with a first-order Fresnel lens. (The station's original five-wick kerosene lamp had been designed by George Meade.) The US Coast Guard decommissioned the light on economic grounds in 1970, replacing it with a simple steel tower erected at the Smyrna Dunes Coast Guard station.

In 1982 the light was restored to active service, primarily because high-rise buildings blocked the Coast Guard's beacon on the other side of the inlet.

The lighthouse and three keepers' dwellings have been restored, and are open to the public seven days a week; the lighthouse tower is also open for climbing.

The original 1867 Barbier et Fenestre first-order fixed lens (installed 1887), and the 1860 Henry Lepaute rotating first-order Fresnel lens, used at the Cape Canaveral Light Station, are on display at the museum.

The 1904 Barbier-Bénard et Turenne rotating third-order Fresnel lens has been restored to service in the tower, which operates today as a private aid to navigation and is maintained by the museum staff.

Pooles Island Light

Aberdeen, MD
Built: 1825
Style: Conical

The Pooles Island Light is the oldest lighthouse still standing in Maryland and the fourth oldest in the Chesapeake Bay area.

Pooles Island was originally called Powell's Island, by John Smith, but over the years the name was changed, possibly to reflect the numerous springs and pools to be found on the island. The island was famed in the 18th and 19th centuries for its fertility, particularly for the peaches raised there in the 1880s and '90s.

Because the island lies near the centre of the bay, near to the mouth of the Gunpowder river, it was one of the first places considered for a lighthouse, and in 1824 Congress appropriated $5000 for construction of a light. John Donahoo and Simon Frieze won the contract to build it, this being the first of many lights constructed by Donahoo. The roughly constructed granite tower and keeper's house were joined three years later by a fog bell tower, the first in the state. In 1857 the original system of Argand lamps and reflectors was replaced by a fourth-order Fresnel lens.

The lighthouse was deactivated in 1939 but remains standing despite being situated in the middle of a bombing range.

In 1994 the army submitted a proposal to designate the lighthouse a National Historic Monument, with the intention of restoring it to service as a private navigational aid. Great efforts were accordingly made to protect and stabilize the structure.

The Pooles Island Light is 'off limits' to the general public because bombing and shelling practice from 1918 through to the early 1960s has left behind unexploded devices.

Port Isabel Light

South Padre Island, TX
Built: 1852
Style: Conical

The Port Isabel Light is an historic building located in Port Isabel, Texas. It was built in 1852 to guide ships through the Brazos Santiago Pass to Port Isabel.

On 28 September 1850, the United States Congress authorized an appropriation of $15,000 for the lighthouse and beacon, and work began in February 1852. Once completed, an 82-ft (25-m) brick tower was revealed, which, by 1854, had 15 lamps and 21 reflectors. A third-order Fresnel lens was installed in 1857, and the fixed light was varied by flashes.

During the American Civil War, the Port Isabel Light was occupied by soldiers from both sides, who used it as a look-out post. After the war, the lighthouse was refitted and returned to operation in 1866. In 1888, the light was temporarily discontinued as claimants proved that the United States government did not have title to the land, forcing the government to condemn it in 1894 to acquire title.

On 15 July 1895, the light was returned to use. It operated for ten years, after which time it was extinguished. On 20 Sept 1927, the government sold the lighthouse and land to a local citizen. In the late 1940s, a movement began to save the lighthouse as an historic site.

On 5 October 1950, the Texas State Park Board accepted the lighthouse and surrounding land as a gift from the owners. It began to restore the lighthouse in 1951, and it was opened to the public in 1952. Today, the lighthouse is operated as a Texas State Historic Site. In September 1996, a new visitors' centre was completed.

Portsmouth Lightship

Built: 1916
Builder: Pusey & Jones, Wilmington, DE
No: LV 101
Length Overall: l0lft 10in (31m)
Beam: 25ft (8m)
Draft: 11ft 4in (3.5m)
Displacement: 360 tons
Illuminating Apparatus: 500-mm lens

The *Portsmouth* is now on permanent display in Portsmouth harbour, Virginia. The vessel was launched in 1916 and served at various hazards off the Delaware, Maryland, Massachusetts and Virginia coasts until it was retired in 1964.

Like other lightships, she was originally known by a number, rather than a name, and although she never served off Portsmouth, she was given that name when first opened to the public in dry dock in Portsmouth harbour in 1986.

Station Assignments
1916–24: Cape Charles (VA)
1925–26: Relief
1926–51: Overfalls (DE)
1951–63: Stonehorse Shoal (MA)

Sand Key Light

Key West, FL
Built: 1827 and 1853
Style: Square pyramidal skeleton tower
No: 1055
Position: 24 27 14 N. 81 52 39 W
Focal plane: 109ft (33m)
Range: 14 miles (22.5km)
Height: 11ft (3.5m)

The Sand Key Light lies 6 nautical miles south-west of Key West, Florida, between the Sand Key and Rock Key Channels, these being two of the channels into Key West.

It is located on a reef that is intermittently covered by sand. At times, the key has been substantial enough to have trees, and in 1900 9,000–12,000 terns were nesting on the island. At other times, however, the island has been completely washed away.

The original Sand Key Light was a brick-built tower dating back to 1827, and one of the first to light the Florida Keys. Its construction was no match for the fierce weather, however, and on 9 October 1846 a hurricane washed both the lighthouse and the island away, killing the keeper and visiting members of his family. A lightship took its place until a replacement tower was built in 1853.

This was a more suitable iron skeleton structure, with a focal plane of 109ft and standing in open water. It was built by George Meade, who anchored the tower to steel pilings driven deep into the coral. The lantern room once held a first-order Fresnel lens, but this was removed when the station was automated in 1941.

The tower was badly damaged by fire in 1989, but has since undergone a $500,000 restoration programme.

Sanibel Island Light

Sanibel Island, FL
Built: 1884
Style: Square pyramidal skeleton tower
No: 1245
Position: 26 27 11 N. 82 00 51 W
Focal plane: 98ft (30m)
Range: 13 miles (21km)
Height: 100ft (30.5m)

The Sanibel Island Light, or Point Ybel Light, was the first lighthouse to be built on Florida's Gulf coast north of Key West and the Dry Tortugas. The lighthouse occupies the eastern tip of Sanibel Island.

Residents of Sanibel Island first petitioned for a lighthouse in 1833, and despite a further recommendation by the Lighthouse Board in 1856, still no action was taken.

Finally, in 1877, government workers made a survey of the eastern end of the island and reserved it for a lighthouse, and Congress finally appropriated funds to build it in 1883. The foundation for the new lighthouse was completed in early 1884, but the ship bringing ironwork for the tower sank 2 miles (3km) from Sanibel Island. Fortunately, divers from Key West recovered all but two of the components meant for the tower.

The purpose of the tower was to guide ships past the dangerous shoals at the entrance to Punta Rassa, its iron-skeleton design allowing storm-driven winds to pass harmlessly through. The skeletal design supports a central cylinder with 127 steps to the lantern room, which once housed a third-order Fresnel lens, although the light is now produced by a modern plastic optic. The tower is accompanied by keepers' cottages, which are built on piles to keep them above the flood tides caused by gales and hurricanes.

The grounds are open to the public, although the lighthouse itself is not.

Seven Foot Knoll Light

Baltimore, MD
Built: 1855
Style: Cylindrical
Position: 39 17 0.96 N. 76 36 19.44 W

The Seven Foot Knoll Light was built in 1855 and is the oldest screwpile lighthouse in Maryland. It was initially installed on a shallow shoal, known as Seven Foot Knoll, at the mouth of the Patapsco river, its purpose being to warn mariners away from a dangerous shoal near the entrance to Baltimore harbour.

Standing on eight iron piles and resembling a large, round, red cheese, the tower was one of the first of its type. The lantern room, on the flat roof of the keeper's dwelling, housed a fourth-order Fresnel lens.

When the station was abandoned after 130 years of service, it was moved to the city of Baltimore, and the 200-ton structure is now a tourist attraction within the Inner Harbor district.

Sharps Island Light

Cambridge, MD
Built: 1838, 1866 and 1882
Style: Conical

The Sharps Island Light, built in 1882, is the third lighthouse to occupy the site, located nearly 3 miles (5km) from the southern end of Tilghman Island in Maryland's Chesapeake Bay. The structure is best-known today for evoking the Leaning Tower of Pisa, an ice floe having caused it to lean in 1977.

The first lighthouse was built on Sharps Island in 1838, but it was moved in 1848 due to erosion of the island. This was replaced by a screwpile lighthouse in 1866, erected very near to the original location of the first structure.

The second lighthouse lasted until 1881 when it was forced off its foundations by an ice floe. It floated nearly 5 miles down the Chesapeake, with its keepers still inside, until it ran aground, allowing the men to escape unharmed.

The current spark-plug lighthouse was constructed in 1882 with a concrete caisson foundation and a 35-ft (10.7-m) cast-iron tower. The fourth-order Fresnel lens was replaced with a 250-mm lens in 1977, the focal plane being 54ft (16.5m) above sea level.

The tower includes an integral dwelling and was manned until 1938, when the United States Coast Guard decided to automate the light. Leaning by about 15°, since it was ice-damaged in 1977, the structure is picturesque despite its poor condition.

The lighthouse is one of the many historic features along the Captain John Smith Chesapeake National Historic Trail.

Sombrero Key Light

Marathon, FL
Built: 1858
Style: Octagonal pyramidal skeleton tower
No: 1000
Position: 24 37 36 N. 81 06 36 W
Focal plane: 142ft (43m)
Range: W 15 miles/24km, R 12 miles/19km
Height: 160ft (49m)

Sombrero Key Light is located near Key Vaca in Marathon, Florida, where it occupies a mostly submerged reef. The name Sombrero Key evokes the Spanish occupation of the area, and old charts show that a small island once existed on the spot. By the later 19th century, however, the island had eroded away, with some parts of the reef becoming exposed at low tide. As a result, the reef and the lighthouse have also been called Dry Banks.

The skeletal lighthouse took four years to erect. Designed and built by Lieutenant George Meade, of the Bureau of Topographical Engineers, it was one of the first galvanized-steel constructions. The tower, completed in 1858, cost $150,000 to build, and the fact that it is still standing, over 150 years later, shows it was well worth the expense.

The tower was originally fitted with a first-order Fresnel lens, but this was replaced by a solar-powered optic when the station was automated in 1984.

St. Augustine Light

St. Augustine, FL
Built: 1824 and 1874
Style: Conical tower
No: 590
Position: 29 53 08 N. 81 17 19 W
Focal plane: 161ft (49m)
Range: F 19 miles/31km, Fl 24 miles/39km
Height: 165ft (50m)

The St. Augustine Light is an active facility at the northern end of Anastasia Island, within the current city limits of St. Augustine.

St. Augustine was the site of the first lighthouse established in Florida by the new territorial American Government in 1824. According to some archival records and maps, this 'official' lighthouse occupied the site of an earlier watchtower, built by the Spanish as early as the late 16th century.

The map of St. Augustine, depicting Sir Francis Drake's attack on the city, by Baptista Boazio, 1589, shows an early wooden watchtower, near to the Spanish structure, which was described as a 'beacon' in Drake's account.

The present 165-ft lighthouse was built in 1874 and towers over Anastasia Island. The brick tower, with its distinctive black-and-white barber's-pole stripes, was built to replace the previous lighthouse, which had collapsed into the sea earlier that year.

The tower still has its original first-order Fresnel lens, despite damage to some of the prisms caused by rifle fire in 1986. Replacements were no longer available, therefore an industrial digitizing process was used to scan the elements that had not been damaged in order to create exact duplicates.

The lighthouse is now maintained as a private aid to navigation and also houses a museum.

St. David's Light

St. David's Island, St. George's Parish,
Bermuda
Built: 1879
Style: Octagonal limestone tower
No: J4472

Focal plane: 196ft (60m)
Range: 23 miles (37km)
Height: 55ft (17m)

The lighthouse was built in 1879 to mark the
easternmost point of Bermuda. Built from local
limestone, the tower stands on Lighthouse
Hill, some 280ft (85m) above the Atlantic. It is
powered by a 1,500-watt electric light bulb
and has a range of 23 miles. The famous red-
and-white-painted tower is the finishing point
for the biennial Newport–Bermuda yacht race.

St. Johns River Light

Mayport, FL
Built: 1830, 1835 and 1859
Style: Conical
Position: 30 23 36.77 N. 81 25 33.49 W

The St. Johns River Light is a decommissioned lighthouse in Jacksonville, Florida, which formerly marked the mouth of the St. Johns river. It is located in the grounds of Naval Station Mayport in the Mayport area.

The St. Johns river has been marked by navigational lights since the first lighthouse was built in 1830. This lasted for just five years before erosion by the sea led to its downfall. Its replacement suffered the opposite problem as sand dunes piled up to a point where they blocked the signal.

The third lighthouse, a 66-ft (20-m) brick-built tower, was raised in 1859 and its third-order Fresnel lens shone out until 1864, when Confederate forces shot out the light.

The tower was relit after the Civil War and an extra 15ft (4.5m) was added to its height in 1887. It remained active until 1929, when the St. John lightship was brought in to replace the light at the mouth of the river. A naval air station has since been built up around the tower, the first 20ft (6m) of which has been encased in a runway extension.

The St. Johns River Light is the oldest surviving building in Mayport, and it has been designated one of the most significant historic buildings in Jacksonville by the Jacksonville Historic Landmarks Commission.

It was added to the National Register of Historic Places in 1976 and underwent restoration in 1980.

St. Marks Light

St. Marks, FL
Built: 1831, 1840 and 1867
Style: White conical tower
No: 10
Position: 30 04 18 N. 84 10 48 W
Focal plane: 82ft (25m)

Range: 8 miles (13km)
Height: 73ft (22m)

The first lighthouse at St. Marks, on the Gulf Coast, was established in 1831, but was so badly constructed that it had to be demolished almost immediately. Its replacement lasted only until 1840, and the third tower was destroyed by gunpowder charges set off by Confederate troops. The present 73-ft lighthouse dates from 1867 and stands on foundations 12ft (3.5m) deep. Although automated, the tower still retains its original fifth-order Fresnel lens.

Turkey Point Light

Elk Neck, MD
Built: 1833
Style: Conical

Turkey Point Light is an historic building at the head of the Chesapeake Bay.

The 38-ft (11.5-m) lighthouse was built in 1833 by John Donohoo. The station's fourth-order Fresnel lens served until the beginning of the 21st century when the lighthouse, made famous by its female keeper, Fanny Salter, was finally decommissioned.

After automation, the tower's remote site made it a target for vandalism. An incident in which the tower was broken into and the lens stolen brought about the removal of a large section of the wooden spiral staircase and the sealing of the entry with a steel door. The keeper's house likewise decayed and was torn down in 1972.

In 2000 the light was decommissioned and turned over to the Turkey Point Light Station Inc., which has taken over the maintenance of the structure; the light was reactivated in 2002. Today, the land around the station is part of Elk Neck State Park.

Tybee Island Light

Tybee Island, GA
Built: 1857 and 1867
Style: Octagonal
Position: 32 1 38.28 N. 80 51 3.24 W

Tybee Island Light is located in Georgia, next to the Savannah river entrance, on the northeast end of Tybee Island. The original lighthouse was built in 1736 and was a wooden tower. It was destroyed in 1741 by a storm, and in 1742, the second lighthouse, made of stone and wood, was finished. In 1773 the third lighthouse was completed and had a brick 100-ft (30-m) tower. The light was refitted with 16-in (406-mm) reflectors in 1841. In 1857 the light was renovated and fitted with a second-order lens.

In 1862, during the American Civil War, the interior of the tower and the lantern were destroyed by fire and the lens was removed. By 1865, the beacon had been relit but not the main light. In 1857 a second-order Fresnel lens was installed. In 1867, a new brick and cast-iron lighthouse was built. The lower 60ft (18m) of the previous light was used as the foundation for the new 144-ft (44-m) lighthouse, and was equipped with a first-order Fresnel lens

In 1869, the Tybee beacon was moved back 165ft (50m) as the site was threatened by storms. In 1871, gales, which had caused great damage along the southern coast, had so greatly damaged the tower that it was reported to be cracked and liable to fall down at any time. The encroachment of the sea upon the southerly point of Tybee Island made it necessary to remove the front beacon, a skeleton-frame structure, and set it back 400ft (120m) on a new foundation in 1873. It had to be moved still further back in 1879.

The lighthouse is open to the public.

Wolf Trap Light

Chesapeake Bay, VA
Built: 1870 and 1893
Style: Octagonal dwelling with square tower
No: 7255
Position: 37 23 24 N. 76 11 24 W
Focal plane: 52ft (16m)
Range: 14 miles (22.5km)

Wolf Trap is a caisson lighthouse in the Virginia portion of the Chesapeake Bay, about 7.5 miles (12km) north-east of New Point Comfort Light.

The first Wolf Trap Light highlighted the problems of screwpile structures in standing up to the pressures of drifting ice. The lighthouse was destroyed during the harsh winter of 1893 and was replaced by the present tower on a concrete and iron caisson later that year. It was fitted with a fourth-order Fresnel lens, which was replaced by a modern optic when the station, which marks the Chesapeake Shoal, where the British warship *Wolf* ran aground in 1691, was automated.

Wolf Trap Light was offered to non-profit-making and historical organizations in 2004 under the National Historic Lighthouse Preservation Act. As no applications were forthcoming, it was put up for auction in 2005. Nick Korstad, of Seattle, Washington, purchased the station, but was unable to obtain financing for his plan to convert the lighthouse into a bed-and-breakfast establishment, and after an unsuccessful attempt to auction the light on e-bay, it was again privately sold.

CHAPTER FIVE

LIGHTHOUSES
OF THE WEST

Alcatraz Light

San Francisco, CA
Built: 1854 and 1909
Style: Octagonal tower
No: 4315
Position: 37 49 36 N. 122 25 18 W
Focal plane: 214ft (65m)
Range: 22 miles (35km)

Alcatraz Island Light, located on Alcatraz Island in the San Francisco Bay, is the oldest light station on the US West Coast. The original tower was built in 1854 in response to a series of shipwrecks in San Francisco Bay during the early days of the Gold Rush.

This first lighthouse was a Cape Cod-style tower and dwelling designed by Francis Gibbons and equipped with a third-order Fresnel lens. In 1858, the island was fortified and these buildings were later converted into a prison.

The earthquake of 1906 damaged both the light tower and the prison, and three years later construction began on a new maximum-security prison and an 84-ft (26-m) octagonal light tower.

In 1915, the station's original Fresnel lens was exhibited at that year's Panama-Pacific Exhibition and the new tower, built outside the prison walls, was re-equipped with a more powerful third-order lens. The light was automated in 1963, six years before the infamous prison was closed.

Shortly after the last prisoner had left, a group of Native Americans occupied the island in a protest and set fire to the keeper's dwelling, which was destroyed.

The lighthouse is now preserved as part of the Golden Gate National Recreational Area and, like the old prison, is open to the public.

Alki Point Light

Seattle, WA
Built: 1887 and 1913
Style: Octagonal tower attached to building
No: 16915
Position: 47 34 35 N. 122 25 14 W
Focal plane: 39ft (12m)
Range: 15 miles (24km)
Height: 37ft (11m)

The Alki Point Light is located at Alki Point, at the southern entrance to Seattle's Elliott Bay.

It began life as a lantern hung on a barn by farmer Hans Martin Hanson, as an aid to vessels heading up Puget Sound towards Seattle. The steady increase in shipping activity during the late 19th century prompted the US Lighthouse Service to pay $15 a month to maintain a lantern and lens, which it installed in 1887. This arrangement continued for a further 26 years until the Coast Guard decided to establish a station on the site in 1913, and the present 37-ft octagonal stone tower was built. This was equipped with a fourth-order Fresnel lens, which was only replaced when the tower was automated, and remains in service today.

Anacapa Islands Light

Anacapa Islands, CA
Built: 1912 and 1932
Style: Cylindrical tower
No: 185
Position: 34 01 06 N. 119 21 36 W
Focal plane: 277ft (84m)
Range: 20 miles (32km)
Height: 55ft (17m)

A lighthouse had been planned on the Anacapa Islands to guide vessels safely through the eastern entrance to the Santa Barbara Channel ever since the steamer *Winfred Scott* ran aground here in 1853, leaving 250 of its passengers stranded.

Despite this incident, Congress remained reluctant to commit the vast sums required to build the light tower in such a remote area, and it was not until 1912 that the first pyramidal steel structure was built on the east side of the Anacapa Islands. This was replaced by the present 55-ft Spanish-style, white cylindrical tower in 1932, which was fitted with a third-order Fresnel lens. The station was automated in 1968 and the Fresnel lens was replaced with a modern optic in 1991.

Battery Point Light

Crescent City, CA
Built: 1856
Style: Two-storey structure
No: 555
Position: 41 44 36 N. 124 12 06 W
Focal plane: 77ft (23.5m)
Range: 14 miles (22.5km)

Battery Point Light, located in Crescent City, California, was one of the first lighthouses on the California coast, where rugged mountains and unbridged rivers meant coastal travel was essential for the economic survival of the region.

In 1855, Congress appropriated $15,000 for the construction of a lighthouse on the tiny islet, which is connected at low tide to Battery Point by an isthmus. Although not included in the 1852 contract by the United States Lighthouse Service for the first eight west-coast lighthouses, the Battery Point Light was actually lit ten days before the Humboldt Harbor Light, the last of the original eight to become operational. The fourth-order Fresnel lens was lit in 1856. The lighthouse was automated in 1953, and a modern 375-mm lens replaced the fourth-order Fresnel lens.

In 1964 the Alaska earthquake, the strongest one ever recorded in the Northern Hemisphere, caused a tsunami. The lighthouse survived, but the following year the modern beacon, that replaced the Fresnel lens in the tower, was switched off, and a flashing light at the end of the nearby breakwater served as the harbor's navigational aid. In 1982, the lighthouse tower was lit again, and the Battery Point Light was listed as a private aid to navigation.

Cape Blanco Light

Port Orford, OR
Built: 1870
Style: Conical tower
No: 595
Position: 42 50 13 N. 124 33 49 W
Focal plane: 245ft (75m)

Range: 26 miles (42km)
Height: 99ft (30m)

Cape Blanco Light, located on Cape Blanco, is Oregon's oldest lighthouse. Built on the 200-ft (61-m) chalk cliffs that gave the cape its name, the 99-ft conical tower, with its attached keeper's cottage, still has its second-order Fresnel lens, giving it a range of 26 miles. The station, which dates back to 1870, was automated in 1980. Twelve years later, the building suffered more than $500,000 worth of damage at the hands of vandals.

Cape Meares Light

Tillamook, OR
Built: 1890
Style: Octagonal
No: 675
Position: 45 29 11 N. 123 58 42 W
Focal plane: 232ft (71m)
Range: 25 miles (40km)
Height: 38ft (11.5m)

Built in 1890, Cape Meares Light served as the light station for Tillamook Bay. When it was built, the lighthouse complex included two keepers' houses, two oil houses, and two cisterns, and was connected to the light by a 1,000-ft (300-m) boardwalk. Later additions included an attached workroom in 1895 and a garage in 1934. The light itself was iron-plated, and due to its exposure to the elements, required frequent repainting over the years. No foghorn was ever installed at Cape Meares. In 1934, the light received electricity, and by now deemed unnecessary, the oil houses were removed.

In 1963, the lighthouse was deactivated and replaced with a newer tower and the Coast Guard made plans to demolish the light. Due to public outcry, however, the plans fell through, and the Coast Guard turned the station over to Tillamook County. The light remained vacant until 1968, when the site was turned over to the Oregon State Parks Department. During this time, vandalism became a major problem where the light was concerned, and it eventually took its toll on the keepers' quarters and they were subsequently demolished. Among the damage, four of the bulls-eyes in the Fresnel lens were stolen. That same year, the light was opened up to the public and the light was restored. Since then, three of the four missing bulls-eyes have been recovered. In 1980, the tower itself was opened to the public.

Cattle Point Light

San Juan Island, WA
Built: 1888 and 1935
Style: Octagonal tower
No: 19555
Position: 48 27 02 N. 122 57 48 W
Focal plane: 94ft (29m)
Range: 7 miles (11km)

San Juan Island is located in San Juan County, in the north-west corner of Washington state. The county is bounded on the west by the Haro Strait, on the east by the Strait of Georgia and Rosario Strait, and on the south by the Strait of Juan de Fuca.

The first light on the island, when the southern end of San Juan Island was a staging post for cattle being shipped to Victoria, British Columbia, was a simple brass lens lantern on a post, which was established in 1888.

The present self-contained octagonal tower was built in 1935 to guide vessels into the San Juan Channel, and continues to be an important aid to navigation.

The Cattle Point Light is located in the Cattle Point Interpretive Area, next to American Camp, a section of the San Juan National Historical Park, on the south-eastern tip of the island. The lighthouse received a temporary makeover in 1984, when it was used as a backdrop for an Exxon television commercial.

Columbia Lightship

Astoria, OR
Built: 1951
Builder: Rice Brothers, East Boothbay, ME
Length overall: 128ft (39m)
Beam: 30ft (9m)
Draft: 11ft (3.5m)
Displacement: 617 tons

Speed: 10.7 knots
Propulsion: Diesel
Illuminating Apparatus: Duplex 500-mm
 electric lens lantern on foremast.
Fog Signal: Twin F2T diaphones aft of pilot
 house; hand-operated bell
Station Assignments:
1951–79: Columbia river (OR)

The *Columbia* lightship was launched in 1951 and spent her active life stationed 8 miles (13km) off the Columbia river bar.

The ship was decommissioned in 1979 and was sold a year later to the Columbia River Maritime Museum in Astoria.

Coquille River Light

Bandon, OR
Built: 1896
Style: Cylindrical

Originally named the Bandon Light, the 40-ft (12-m) white stucco Coquille River Light was commissioned in 1895, and was first lit on 29 February 1896, its purpose being to guide mariners past the dangerous shifting sandbars into the Coquille river and harbour at Bandon.

The lighthouse was connected to the nearby keeper's house by a wooden walkway. The station was badly damaged by fire in 1939 and the tower lay abandoned until a restoration project was launched by the state. The work was undertaken by the US Corps of Engineers and the brick-built tower is now a tourist attraction within Bullards Beach State Park. The light's fourth-order Fresnel lens was replaced by a jetty light and series of buoys, but since its restoration, the tower has been relit to shine its light inland.

Diamond Head Light

Oahu Island, HI
Built: 1899 and 1917
Style: Concrete tower
No: 29060
Position: 21 15 18 N. 157 48 36 W
Focal plane: 147ft (45m)
Range: W 17 miles/27km, R 14 miles/23km
Height: 55ft (17m)

The Diamond Head Light is located on the island of Oahu in the state of Hawaii.

The present lighthouse was built in 1917 to replace a similarly-sized square masonry tower that had marked the entrance to Honolulu harbour since 1899.

The present tower, built in 1917, was constructed of reinforced concrete and stands 55ft high. The original ironwork of the watchroom and lantern are still in use, the original lighting equipment being a 3rd-order Fresnel lens and a special multiple-wick kerosene oil lamp, imported from France in 1899.

The lighthouse was automated in 1924 and the keeper's dwelling is now the official residence of the Commander of the Coast Guard's 14th District.

Eldred Rock Light

Haines, AK
Built: 1906
Style: Octagonal tower on building
No: 23880
Position: 58 58 15 N. 135 13 15 W
Focal plane: 91ft (28m)

Range: 8 miles (13m)

The Eldred Rock Light is an historic octagonal building standing adjacent to the Lynn Canal in Alaska. It is the last of the ten lighthouses constructed in that state between 1902 and 1906. The 56-ft (17-m) lighthouse was built in 1906 to guide vessels into the Lynn Canal following the sinking of the *Clara Nevada* with the loss of 100 lives and $100,000-worth of gold eight years earlier. The station retains its original fourth-order Fresnel lens and was automated in 1973.

Grays Harbor Light

Westport, WA
Built: 1898
Style: Truncated octagonal pyramid tower
No: 720
Position: 46 53 18 N. 124 07 01 W
Focal plane: 123ft (37.5m)
Height: 107ft (33m)

The Grays Harbor Light, dedicated in 1898, is the tallest lighthouse in Washington and the third tallest on North America's west coast. It marks the entrance to Grays Harbor, which is one of Washington's few outer-coast harbours.

Officials of the Thirteenth Lighthouse District selected a site for the lighthouse facing the Pacific Ocean, about 400ft (122m) from the water's edge. Massive amounts of accretion, however, due mainly to the jetty system at the entrance to Grays Harbor, have since built up, and the lighthouse currently stands approximately 3,000ft (915m) from high tide.

Construction of the Grays Harbor Light began in 1897, the base of the lighthouse resting on a 12-ft (4-m) foundation of sandstone. Its walls, which are 4ft (1.2m) thick at the base, are made of brick with a coating of cement on the exterior.

In August 1992, the original third-order Fresnel lens was extinguished and a smaller light, manufactured in New Zealand, was mounted on the balcony. The lantern room, however, still holds the original Fresnel lens. The new light operates on a 35-watt bulb and can be seen for 19 miles (31km) on the white sector, 17 on the red.

Visitors can tour the lighthouse, which is operated by the Westport South Beach Historical Society. In 1977, the lighthouse achieved listing on the National Register of Historic Places.

Heceta Head Light

Florence, OR
Built: 1894
Style: Conical tower
No: 635
Position: 44 08 15 N. 124 07 42 W
Focal plane: 205ft (62m)
Range: 28 miles (45km)
Height: 65ft (20m)

Heceta Head Light is located on the Oregon coast 13 miles (21km) north of Florence, and 13 miles (21km) south of Yachats, Oregon. It is located at the Heceta Head Lighthouse State Scenic Viewpoint (a state park), midway up a 205-ft (63-m) tall headland. Built in 1894, the lighthouse emits a beam visible for 28 miles, making it the strongest light on the Oregon coast.

The construction of the lighthouse was a logistical nightmare. The site was midway along a 90-mile (145-km) stretch of remote coastline between Cape Foulweather and Cape Arago, and the materials had to be shipped to the Siuslaw river before being hauled overland by wagon to Heceta Head.

The project took two years to complete at a cost of $180,000. The 65-ft tower, which stands 205ft (62m) above sea level, was equipped originally with a five-wick oil lamp illuminated by a 640-prism first-order Fresnel lens. The light is now electrically powered but the Fresnel lens was retained when the station was automated in 1963.

The keeper's quarters are reputed to be haunted by the ghost of an elderly woman, nicknamed Rue. Several incidents have been reported, including visible apparitions, moved objects, and occasional housekeeping. Most reported sightings of Rue occur in the attic, with many having seen her from the outside when looking up into the attic.

Kilauea Point Light

Kauai Island, HI
Built: 1913
Style: Conical

The 53-ft (16-m) Kilauea Point Light was built on the north side of Kauai Island in 1913 to mark the northernmost point in the Hawaiian Island chain. Standing on the top of high cliffs, the tower's second-order Fresnel lens had a focal plane of 216ft (66m). The lighthouse was manned until the station was decommissioned in 1976.

In 1985 the Kilauea Point National Wildlife Refuge started with the original Coast Guard Station, and then expanded to preserve the surrounding habitat. A new visitor centre was built in 1988, operated by the Kilauea Point Natural History Association. Starting in late 2008, the group now raise funds for the restoration of the lighthouse.

The buildings were damaged by Hurricane Iniki in September 1992, but were fortunately repaired.

Lime Kiln Light

San Juan Island, WA
Built: 1914
Style: Octagonal tower attached to building
No: 19695
Position: 48 31 00 N. 123 09 12 W
Focal plane: 55ft (17m)
Range: 17 miles (27km)

Height: 38ft (11.5m)

The Lime Kiln Light was built on San Juan Island in 1914 to serve vessels bound for the Roche Harbor Lime & Cement Company.

Appropriately, the tower is of concrete construction and was one of the last major stations to be built in Washington state. It was also the last to be electrified, having relied instead on oil-vapour incandescent lamps to illuminate a 375-mm prismatic lens until it was updated during World War II.

The light station, which overlooks Haro Strait and Dead Man's Bay, is close to a main migratory route for whales and now houses a whale research centre.

Makapu'u Point Light

Waimanalo, Oahu Island, HI
Built: 1929
Style: Cylindrical concrete tower
No: 28925
Position: 21 18 36 N. 157 38 54 W
Focal plane: 420ft (128m)
Range: 19 miles (30.5km)
Height: 46ft (14m)

The Makapu'u Point Light, on the island of Oahu, has the largest lens of any lighthouse in the United States. Twelve miles (19km) east of Honolulu, it is a popular hiking spot, offering great views of Makapu'u and Waimanalo Bay on one side and the Ka Iwi Channel on the other. The lighthouse also makes a good vantage point from which to view whales, and the rocky cliffs are popular with hang-gliders.

The lighthouse was built in 1929 to mark the eastern point of Oahu Island and guide vessels from the United States towards the port of Honolulu. Perched on a lava ledge more than 380ft (116m) above the Pacific Ocean, the lighthouse can boast the largest Fresnel lens in North America, having a diameter of 8ft 6in (2.5m). A 12-ft (3.5m) radio beacon was added and the station was automated in 1974.

The lighthouse sits high on a volcanic point, overlooking cerulean blue seas and has been described as 'one of the most breathtaking coastal panoramas of any in the United States'. The lighthouse, and the area surrounding it, is owned by the US Coast Guard.

Mukilteo Light

Elliott Point, Mukilteo, WA

Built: 1906

Style: Octagonal tower attached to building

No: 18460

Position: 47 56 55 N. 122 18 22 W

Focal plane: 33ft (10m)

Range: 14 miles (22.5km)

Height: 30ft (9m)

The attractive, wood-framed Mukilteo Light was built in 1906 to guide vessels through the Puget Sound towards the port of Everett. The tower still retains its original fourth-order Fresnel lens, thanks in part to protests from locals opposing plans by the Coast Guard to replace the lamp with an aero-marine beacon in 1990.

New Dungeness Light

New Dungeness, WA
Built: 1857
Style: Conical tower on dwelling
No: 16335
Position: 48 10 54 N. 123 06 37 W
Focal plane: 67ft (20.5m)

Range: 18 miles (29km)
Height: 63ft (19m)

The New Dungeness Light was built in 1857 to guide vessels through the Strait of Juan de Fuca into the Puget Sound. It also warns of the dangerous spit of moving sand protruding from New Dungeness, which a storm in 1871 turned into an island for a time.

The tower, which was fitted with a third-order Fresnel lens, once stood 89ft (27m) high, but was later lowered to 63ft. The station was automated in 1976 but is still manned by volunteer keepers.

North Head Light
Ilwaco, WA
Built: 1898
Style: Conical tower
No: 700
Position: 46 17 56 N. 124 04 41 W
Focal plane: 194ft (59m)

Range: 26 miles (42km)
Height: 65ft (20m)

The lighthouse stands in one of the windiest regions of the country on cliffs overlooking the entrance to the Columbia river. The sandstone tower was built in 1898 as a result of a series of shipwrecks on Long Beach peninsula. It was originally equipped with a first-order Fresnel lens transferred from the lighthouse on Cape Disappointment, north of what is now Fort Canby State Park. This lens was later replaced by an aero-beacon, which gives the light a range of 26 miles.

Old Point Loma Light

San Diego, CA
Built: 1855
Style: Skeletal tower

The Old Point Loma Light was built in 1855 to mark the entrance to San Diego harbour and was one of the first on the west coast. The 40-ft (12-m) tower, and its Cape Cod-style dwelling, stands 460ft (140m) above sea level.

Its third-order lens had a range of 40 miles (64km), but only on clear nights, for in bad weather or foggy conditions the light shone above the cloud base and proved worse than useless. The station was decommissioned in 1891 and replaced by a skeletal tower situated on the tip of Point Loma. In 1963, the original tower and its buildings were transformed into a museum managed by the National Park Service.

Piedras Blancas Light

Cambria, CA
Built: 1875 and 1949
Style: Flat-topped conical tower
No: 265
Position: 35 39 56 N. 121 17 04 W
Focal plane: 142ft (43m)
Range: 21 miles (34km)

The Piedras Blancas Light Station stands on Point Piedras Blancas, about 5.5 miles (9km) north-west of San Simeon, California. It is named for a white, rocky out-cropping, located just off the end of the point. This location was chosen in 1866 to fill the gap between the lighthouses at Point Conception and Point Sur.

The first-order Fresnel lens, on the 106-ft (32-m) lighthouse, was first illuminated in 1875. On 31 December 1948 and 1 January 1949, three earthquakes of a magnitude of 3.8–4.6 occurred 6 miles (10km) off the point, damaging the lantern room. The lens, lantern room, ornate railing, and the upper portion of the tower were removed, reducing the height of the tower to 74ft (23m). The lens is now on display in the nearby community of Cambria.

The United States Coast Guard staffed the light station until 1975 when the tower was automated and the station left unmanned. The light is an active aid to navigation even though the sound signal has now been silenced. The site is currently maintained by the United States Department of the Interior Bureau of Land Management.

The Bureau of Land Management has assumed administrative control and is in the process of initiating restoration and stabilization of the building and, to this end, the bureau has completed a planning framework that will guide these activities.

Pigeon Point Light

Pescadero, CA
Built: 1872
Style: Conical tower
No: 320
Position: 37 10 54 N. 122 23 36 W
Focal plane: 148ft (45m)
Range: 24 miles (39km)

Height: 115ft (35m)

Pigeon Point was built to guide ships towards San Francisco. The lighthouse stands on imposing cliffs, 160ft (49m) above the Pacific swell. The point was given its name in memory of the lives lost when the American clipper, *Pigeon*, foundered on these rocks in 1853. Another vessel to founder here, 12 years later, was the British ship, *Sir John Franklin*, which ran onto the rocks directly below the point where the lighthouse now stands; all hands were lost. The lighthouse was automated in 1974 and its light was replaced with an aero-beacon. The tower and its buildings now double as a youth hostel.

Point Arena Light

Point Arena, CA
Built: 1870 and 1908
Style: Cylindrical tower
No: 420
Position: 38 57 17 N. 123 44 26 W
Focal plane: 155ft (47m)
Range: 25 miles (40km)
Height: 115ft (35m)

The Point Arena Light is located in Mendocino County, California, 2 miles (3km) north of Point Arena.

Standing astride the San Andreas Fault, when the infamous 1906 earthquake levelled much of San Francisco, Point Arena suffered only minor damage, apart from its brick-built lighthouse of 1870, which was left with a large crack. This led to the first 'earthquake-proof' concrete lighthouse being built here in 1908; the success of the design of its tower led to others being built in areas prone to seismic activity, including other parts of California, Hawaii and Alaska.

The lighthouse features a small museum and giftshop. Guided tours of the light station, as well as self-guided tours of the grounds, are available daily.

196

Point Bonita Light

San Francisco, CA
Built: 1855 and 1877
Style: Tower on building
No: 370
Position: 37 48 54 N. 122 31 48 W
Focal plane: 124ft (38m)
Range: 18 miles (29km)
Height: 33ft (10m)

The original lighthouse was built in 1855 to mark a narrow manoeuvring area within what are now called the Golden Gate Straits. Like so many other early lighthouses in this region, the 56-ft (17-m) brick tower was built too high to be effective in the foggy conditions that often affect the area. The US Army attempted to resolve the problem by setting up a cannon on the site, and a 1,500-lb (680-kg) fog bell was installed later on. Neither proved effective, so work began in 1872 to construct the present tower lower down the cliff, the project taking five years to complete.

In 1940 a landslide carried away the bridge linking the station with the mainland, and it was eventually replaced by a suspension bridge.

Point Cabrillo Light

Mendocino, CA
Built: 1909
Style: Octagonal frame tower on building
No: 450
Position: 39 20 54 N. 123 49 36 W
Focal plane: 81ft (25m)

Range: 22 miles (35km)
Height: 47ft (14m)

Point Cabrillo Light, and its Cape Cod-style station, became one of the most popular postings within the Coast Guard service. The lighthouse, which stands 50ft (15m) above the Pacific, was equipped with a third-order Fresnel lens, replaced with an aero-beacon when the light was automated.

The site is now managed by California Coastal Conservancy, and is one of 70 state parks scheduled for closure in 2012, due to state budget cuts.

Point Conception Light

Santa Barbara Channel, CA

Built: 1856 and 1882

Style: Cylindrical tower behind building

No: 200

Position: 34 26 54 N. 120 28 12 W

Focal plane: 133ft (40.5m)

Range: 26 miles (42km)

Height: 52ft (16m)

The original Point Conception Light, built in 1856, was one of the first stations to be established on the west coast.

Unfortuately, it suffered not only from a catalogue of construction disasters, including being too small to accept the first-order Fresnel lens allotted to the tower, but also from being built too high up to be effective in foggy conditions. The tower was finally abandoned in 1882 after the present 52-ft cylindrical tower was erected lower down this hazardous stretch of cliffs. The station was automated in 1973.

The lighthouse was moved in 1881 to where fog would be less likely to obscure the light, and was rebuilt from the top of the bluff to a mesa halfway down, at a height of 133ft (41m) above the Pacific Ocean.

Point Fermin Light

San Pedro, CA
Built: 1874
Style: Square, skeletal tower

The original Point Fermin Light was built in 1874 on Paseo Del Mar to guide shipping towards San Pedro harbour. The square redwood tower and attached keeper's dwelling is in the same Italianate design as its twin at Point Hueneme, farther north.

It was equipped with a fourth-order Fresnel lens until World War II, when all lighthouses were subject to security blackout. At Cape Firmin, however, the tower suffered the ignominy of having its lantern room removed and replaced with a watchtower, which transformed it into something locals thought resembled a chicken coop. When peace resumed, the lighthouse was replaced with a skeletal steel tower built on the edge of the cliffs. The original lighthouse has now been fully restored and is a tourist attraction within Point Fermin City Park.

Point Hueneme Light

Oxnard, CA
Built: 1874 and 1941
Style: Square tower on building
No: 190
Position: 34 08 43 N. 119 12 36 W
Focal plane: 52ft (16m)
Range: 20 miles (32km)
Height: 48ft (15m)

Point Hueneme Light, on the northern side of the eastern entrance to the Santa Barbara Channel, is a buff-coloured Art Deco-style tower on a fog-signal building. It replaced an older structure established in 1874.

The first lighthouse was built to mark the Santa Barbara Channel in the same year as its twin tower at Point Fermin. The original tower, which was sold in 1941 and later pulled down, was replaced by the present Art Deco square tower, 48ft in height, with an integrated fog-signal building, and was fitted with a fourth-order Fresnel lens. The station was automated in 1972.

The lighthouse is federal property, owned and operated by the United States Coast Guard.

In March 2008, the city of Port Hueneme and Oxnard Harbor District dedicated a new 'Ligthouse Promenade', beginning at the Hueneme Sunset Beach and following the perimeter fence of the port to the lighthouse. The half-mile promenade is on a flat, even surface and allows visitors to take a leisurely stroll along the beach. There are no public restrooms on the property, the nearest public facilities being at the promenade's entrance at Sunset Beach.

The Point Hueneme Light is open for tours on the third Saturday of each month, February through to October. The hours are 10:00am to 3:00pm, and admission to the lighthouse is free.

Point Loma Light

San Diego, CA
Built: 1891
Style: Square pyramidal skeleton tower
No: 5
Position: 32 39 54 N. 117 14 34 W

Focal plane: 88ft (27m)
Range: 22 miles (35km)
Height: 70ft (21m)

The 70-ft Point Loma Light was erected in 1891 to replace the old light station built 36 years earlier high above the fog banks that sometimes shroud San Diego harbour. The cast-iron skeletal tower, which stands 88ft (27m) above sea level, has a third-order Fresnel lens, which was borrowed for display at the 1893 World Exposition in Chicago.

Point Montara Light

Pacifica, CA
Built: 1900 and 1926
Style: Conical tower
No: 335
Position: 37 32 12 N. 122 31 12 W
Focal plane: 70ft (21m)
Range: 15 miles (24km)
Height: 30ft (9m)

The present 30-ft Point Montara Light was built to replace a beacon once sited over an offshore ledge, north of Half Moon Bay, which had been occasioned by the loss of the steamer *Colorado* in 1868 and the freighter *Acuelo* three years later.

The current tower was first erected in 1881 in Wellfleet, Massachusetts, as the Mayo Beach Light. In 1925, the cast-iron tower from the discontinued Mayo Beach Light was disassembled and moved to Yerba Buena. It was rebuilt as the Point Montara Light in 1928, where it stands today.

The station's original fourth-order Fresnel lens had a range of 15 miles, but it was replaced with a modern optic when the tower was automated in 1970. The station now doubles as a youth hostel.

Point No Point Light

Hansville, WA
Built: 1880
Style: Octagonal tower on building
No: 16550
Position: 47 54 44 N. 122 31 37 W
Focal plane: 27ft (8m)
Range: 17 miles (27km)
Height: 20ft (6m)

Occupying Point No Point, on the west side of Puget Sound, near the point where Admiralty Inlet ends, in the small town of Hansville, the Point No Point Light is the oldest lighthouse on Puget Sound. Built in 1880, it is a sister tower to the West Point Light, built a year later on the opposite side of Puget Sound to mark the entrance to Elliott Bay and the port of Seattle.

It was equipped with a bull's-eye fourth-order Fresnel lens, giving the 20-ft tower a range of 17 miles, but its presence did not prevent the *Admiral Sampson* from colliding with the liner *Princess Victoria* off the point in 1914, a disaster that led to the loss of 12 lives.

In 1997, the last US Coast Guard personnel left Point No Point and it stood empty until the Coast Guard leased the property to Kitsap County Parks and Recreation.

Point Pinos Light

Pacific Grove, CA
Built: 1855
Style: Tower on dwelling
No: 290
Position: 36 38 00 N. 121 56 00 W
Focal plane: 89ft (27m)
Range: 17 miles (27km)
Height: 43ft (13m)

The Point Pinos Light was built in 1855 on the southern tip of Monterey Bay, and is the oldest active lighthouse on the west coast.

Designed by Francis Gibbons, the Cape Cod-style station still has its original third-order Fresnel lens. The granite tower was one of many damaged during the 1906 San Francisco earthquake, but it was successfully repaired using reinforced concrete.

The present light source is a 1-kilowatt bulb, which produces a 50,000-candela beam visible under favourable conditions for up to 17 miles. Formerly, the light was lit one hour prior to sunset and extinguished one hour after sunrise, but with automation completed in 1975, a small battery-operated back-up strobe light was installed outside the tower, and the main light was turned on permanently.

Point Robinson Light

Maury Island, WA
Built: 1885 and 1915
Style: Octagonal tower
No: 17070
Position: 42 23 17 N. 122 22 28 W
Focal plane: 40ft (12m)
Range: 13 miles (21km)

The 38-ft (11.5-m) tall Point Robinson Light is located at Point Robinson, on the coast of the Puget Sound in the state of Washington, Point Robinson being the most easterly point of Maury Island.

The Point Robinson station began life in 1885 as a fog-signal station to warn vessels away from a dangerous spit of sand that extends into Puget Sound. By 1915, traffic through this narrow waterway had increased significantly, and the Lighthouse Board built the present masonry tower alongside the fog-signal building. In 2008, the Coast Guard replaced the original Fresnel light with a replaceable plastic beacon mounted outside the lantern room, but the original Fresnel lens remains in the lantern room where it can be viewed by visitors.

Point Sur Light

Big Sur, CA
Built: 1889
Style: Tower on stone building
No: 280
Position: 36 18 24 N. 121 54 06 W

Point Sur was built on one of the most rugged sections of the west coast, between Big Sur and Monterey. It took nine years to persuade Congress to agree to the siting of a lighthouse in this remote area and another four years to complete the project, which ended up costing twice the original budget.

Engineers first had to build a railroad to transport the materials, then cut 395 steps down the steep sandy bluff where the 50-ft (15-m) tower was erected. The lighthouse was equipped with a first-order Fresnel lens with a focal plane of 250ft (76m) above the Pacific. The station had a range of 25 miles (40km). When the tower was automated in 1972, the Fresnel lens was exchanged for an aero-beacon.

Life on Point Sur was very isolated, the only road, which led to Monterey, being long and often dangerous. The keepers received goods and bulk supplies by boat roughly every four months. A 'lighthouse tender' brought the supplies, but to get them ashore, the supplies were transferred to skiffs and floated to land in barrels.

State Highway 1 was built along the coast, and life on the Point Sur became less isolated. The light was automated by the United States Coast Guard in 1972. The original Fresnel lens was moved to the Maritime Museum of Monterey, where it is currently on display.

In 1991, the old lighthouse and a 37-acre (15-hectare) area was listed on the US National Register of Historic Places as the Point Sur Light Station.

Point Vicente Light

Rancho Palos Verdes, CA
Built: 1926
Style: Cylindrical
Position: 33 44 30.84 N. 118 24 38.16 W

The Point Vicente Light is located north of Los Angeles harbour, California.

The 67-ft (20-m) lighthouse was built in 1926 on a 100-ft (30.5-m) cliff overlooking the Pacific at Rancho Palos Verdes. The tower has been the backdrop for a number of Hollywood epics, and because of this film publicity has become one of California's most easily recognizable landmarks. The lighthouse still has its original third-order Fresnel lens, which has a range of 20 miles (32km). The tower was automated in 1973.

Point Wilson Light

Port Townsend, WA
Built: 1879 and 1914
Style: Octagonal tower on building
No: 16475
Position: 48 08 39 N. 122 45 17 W
Focal plane: 51ft (15.5m)
Range: W 16 miles/26km, R 15 miles/24km

Point Wilson is a finger of land jutting into the sea where the Strait of Juan de Fuca meets Puget Sound in Washington state. Located near Port Townsend, the Point Wilson Light is an important navigational aid to ships travelling to Seattle and other ports in the Puget Sound.

To passing ships, the lighthouse appears on the starboard side and marks the place where they must make a right turn to enter Admiralty Inlet if their destination is the Puget Sound.

Each lighthouse has its own signal to help ship captains determine their location: the signal coming from the Point Wilson beacon is a white light which is on for 15 seconds, then off for 5 seconds, with one red flash during the time that it is off.

The original lighthouse was built at Point Wilson in 1879 and its light was visible for up to 13 miles (21km). The current lighthouse is 49ft (15m) tall and was built in 1914 to replace the original wooden structure, but the earlier lighthouse remained as the light keeper's house. The light was fitted with a fourth-order Fresnel lens. The station, which is now automated, is equipped with a fog signal and radio beacon.

Several people, who have spent time in the keeper's house, have reported paranormal activities, including sightings of shadowy figures, sounds like someone walking on the second floor, and objects being mysteriously moved.

San Luis Obispo Light

San Luis Obispo, CA
Built: 1890 and 1976
Style: Tower on cylindrical structure
No: 225
Position: 35 09 36 N. 120 45 36 W

Focal plane: 116ft (35m)
Range: 20 miles (32km)

The original 40-ft (12-m) San Luis Opispo Light was built in 1890 on a remote headland that could only be serviced from the sea.

Standing 130ft (40m) above sea level, the square tower was equipped with a fourth-order Fresnel lens. The station was automated in 1975, and was replaced the following year by a cylindrical tower fitted with an aero-marine beacon.

Santa Cruz Light/Mark Abbott Memorial Light

Santa Cruz, CA
Built: 1870, 1948 and 1967
Style: Square tower attached to building
No: 305
Position: 36 57 06 N. 122 01 36 W

Focal plane: 60ft (18m)
Range: 17 miles (27km)
Height: 39ft (12m)

The original lighthouse was built in 1870 to guide lime and lumber ships in and out of this logging port.

The 35-ft (10.5-m) wood and brick lighthouse, equipped with a fifth-order Fresnel lens, was pulled down after World War II. The present 39-ft lighthouse was built in 1967 as a memorial to Mark Abbott, a surfer who drowned nearby. The building serves as a surfing museum.

Swiftsure Lightship

Northwest Seaport, Seattle, WA
Built: 1904
Builder: New York Shipbuilding Co.
 Camden, NJ
No. 83
Design: Steam screw; steel hull; two steel
 masts; stack amidships
Length overall: 129ft (39m)
Beam: 28ft 6in (9m)
Draft: 12ft 6in (4m)
Displacement: 668 tons
Propulsion: Steam
Speed: 9 knots
Illuminating Apparatus: Three oil lens
 lanterns raised to each masthead

Lightship Number 83, now called *Swiftsure*, was launched in Camden, New Jersey, in 1904 and is now moored in Seattle, Washington. She steamed around the tip of South America to her first station at Blunts Reef, in California, where she saved 150 people when their ship ran aground in dense fog.

Formerly known as *Relief*, Number 83 has had numerous names on her sides, all of which indicated the location of her station, *Swiftsure* referring to the Swiftsure Bank, near the entrance to the Strait of Juan de Fuca, which separates Washington from Vancouver Island. She also guided ships near Umatilla Reef and the Columbia river bar.

Swiftsure is one of the oldest lightships in the country and the only one to have her original steam engines. She is 129ft long, with a displacement of 668 tons. Her aids to navigation include a 1,000-watt primary light, a 140-decibel Diaphone horn, and a 1,000-lb (454-kg) foredeck fog bell.

The ship was decommissioned in 1960, and was purchased by Northwest Seaport in 1969.

Tillamook Rock Light

Seaside, OR
Built: 1881
Style: Square

The 150-ft (46-m) Tillamook Rock Light, which marks the southern approaches to the Columbia river, is one of America's most enduring structures. Built in 1881 on a wind- and wave-swept rock, 'Terrible Tilly', as keepers called the tower, is often dwarfed by the waves of the 'Pineapple Express' – the winter storms that blow up from the South Pacific. One engineer lost his life during the two-year construction, and at times, when conditions were too rough to land a boat, it was necessary to take the keepers in and out by breeches buoy.

In 1883, rocks thrown up by the waves smashed through the iron dome in 20 places, and 11 years later the lantern room was breeched by waves, bringing in fish, rocks and seaweed, which shattered 13 glass panels in the station's first-order Fresnel lens. The lighthouse was finally replaced by an automated buoy in 1957 and was owned by the burial group, Eternity by the Sea, which used the lighthouse as a final resting place for people's ashes. After interring about 30 urns, the columbarium's licence was revoked in 1999 by the Oregon Mortuary and Cemetery Board and was rejected upon reapplication in 2005.

Trinidad Head Light

Trinidad, CA
Built: 1871
Style: Square tower
No: 525
Position: 41 03 06 N. 124 09 06 W
Focal plane: 196ft (60m)
Range: 14 miles (22.5km)
Height: 20ft (6m)

The Trinidad Head Light, located in Trinidad Harbor, California, is an historic site situated 20 miles (32km) north of Eureka, California.

The lighthouse was built in 1871 on a headland standing more than 170ft (52m) above the Pacific. Despite the height, waves have been known to break right over the station; in 1913 the lighthouse keeper reported that the tower and balcony were awash.

In 1947, a modern optic and air horn replaced the Fresnel lens and fog bell, and the US Coast Guard replaced the keeper's residences by a triplex in the late 1960s. Today, the station is automated. A replica of the tower was built overlooking the bay by the Trinidad Civic Club, which houses the original Fresnel lens. The bell is displayed nearby.

Umpqua River Light

Winchester Bay, OR
Built: 1856 and 1894
Style: Conical tower
No: 620
Position: 43 39 42 N. 124 11 54 W
Height: 65ft (20m)

The Umpqua River Light is situated on the Oregon coast at the mouth of the Umpqua river on Winchester Bay, in Douglas County.

The first lighthouse was completed after there had been an odd contretemps with the local people, who had appropriated the workers' tools.

Built along the river channel, the original lighthouse of 1856 was vulnerable to seasonal flooding, which led to yearly erosion of the sand embankment on which it stood. A flood then undermined the station during the winter of 1862, and the lighthouse collapsed while workmen were removing its first-order Fresnel lens.

By October 1863, the building's foundations had become too unstable, but the Light House Board had foreseen the need to build a new light at the location, although it was 1888 before Congress approved of a construction of a new lighthouse.

With the erection of the nearby Cape Arago Light, the site was abandoned until 1894, when the present 65-ft conical tower, equipped with another first-order Fresnel lens, was built. The light stands 165ft (50m) above sea level and was automated in 1966.

Visitors can tour the lighthouse and adjacent Coastal History Museum from May through to September. The museum is located in an historic US Coast Guard station and features exhibits relevant to the lighthouse, to local history and to the history of the US Coast Guard on the Umpqua river.

Warrior Rock Light

Sauvie Island, OR
Built: 1889
Style: White pyramidal structure
No: 11060
Position: 45 50 55 N. 122 47 18 W
Range: 7 miles (11km)

The existing Warrior Rock Light, built in 1889, was originally a small two-storey structure atop a sandstone foundation, the first floor, with its single room, serving as the keeper's quarters. The second floor was primarily a covered half-deck housing the lens lantern and fog bell. Eventually, a house and barn were added to the property.

The fog bell has the distinction of being the oldest in the Pacific North-West.

In the 1930s, the little frame lighthouse was replaced with a 28-ft concrete tower, built on the same square sandstone foundation. There it remained until 27 May 1969, when a barge ran into the lighthouse causing considerable damage to the foundation and disabling the light and fog bell.

While the US Coast Guard debated whether or not to rebuild the tower, the historic bell was removed. During the move, the bell fell into the river and was severely cracked; it was never returned to the lighthouse.

Today, only the automated light stands at the point, the bungalow having burned down in the early 1990s. The fog bell is now on display in front of the St. Helens Courthouse, while a half-size replica of the original lighthouse can also be seen to the courthouse's rear in Columbia View Park.

Yaquina Head Light

Newport, OR
Built: 1873
Style: Conical tower
No: 650
Position: 44 40 36 N. 124 04 48 W
Focal plane: 162ft (49m)
Range: 19 miles (30.5km)
Height: 93ft (28m)

The brick-built Yaquina Head Light is another of Oregon's lighthouses to have been sited, like Cape Meares, in the wrong location. It ended up at Newport instead of Cape Foulweather after a mapmaker erroneously transposed the two points on a US Coast Guard survey chart.

One of the most attractive lighthouses in North America, Yaquina Head sits on a bed of heavily magnetized iron which causes wide deviation on ships' compasses, a local phenomenon that led to several shipwrecks, including that of one vessel that was carrying parts intended for the light's original first-order Fresnel lens.

The station was automated in 1966, and is now maintained by Oregon State Parks.

Baccaro Point Light

Barrington Bay, NS
Built 1851 and 1934
Style: Square pyramidal wooden tower
No: H3782
Position: 43 26 58 N. 65 28 17 W
Focal plane: 52ft (16m)
Range: 16 miles (26km)
Height: 45ft (14m)

Baccaro is the oldest place name in Nova Scotia, and comes from the Basque word, *baccolaos* (cod-fish). The point is one of the major headlands of the South Shore, making it one of the best places in Nova Scotia to view birds normally seen only when at sea; these include northern gannets, jaegers and sooty shearwaters. There are also panoramic views east to the Dalvages Light and west to Nova Scotia's tallest light on Cape Sable Island.

The first Baccaro Point Light was a three-storey structure with the lantern extending from the roof. It was built in 1851 to guide vessels towards Port La Tour in Barrington Bay. Seal oil was used to fuel the light until 1865, when the station was upgraded to kerosene burners.

In 1934, the building burned down and was replaced by the present 45-ft tower with its red octagonal iron lantern. The old keeper's dwelling was pulled down when the station was automated in 1984.

Baddeck Light

Cape Breton Island, NS
Built: 1875
Style: Square pyramidal wooden tower

The Baddeck Light, also known as the Kidston Island Light, is located at the northeastern tip of Kidston Island and is a well-known landmark.

It was established in 1875 as an aid to navigation on the Bras d'Or Lake, and can be reached by boat or viewed from the shore.

The Baddeck Light is one of three lighthouses on Cape Breton Island and is part of the Cabot Trail, which also includes the other lighthouses at Chéticamp and Peggy's Point.

Brier Island Light
Digby Neck, NS
Built: 1809, 1832 and 1944
Style: Octagonal concrete tower
No: H3872
Position: 44 14.9 N. 66 23.5 W
Focal plane: 95ft (29m)

Range: 17 miles (27km)
Height: 60ft (18m)

Brier Island Light was one of the first to be built in Canada. A light was recorded on what locals call West Point as early as 1809 to guide vessels into St. Mary's Bay.

A 55-ft (17-m) wooden lighthouse was erected in 1832 and burned down in 1944, when it was replaced by the present 60-ft concrete tower.

Shortly after, three red daymark stripes were added to the previously all white tower to make it more visible in snowy weather.

Brockton Point Light

Vancouver Harbour, BC
Built: 1890, 1901 and 1914
Style: Square tower, octagonal lantern
No: G5447
Position: 49 18.1 N. 123 06.6 W
Focal plane: 40ft (12m)
Range: 11 miles (18km)
Height: 29ft 6in (9m)

The Brockton Point Light began life in 1890 as red-and-white lanterns attached to a pole. It marked the sharp turn into Coal Harbour for vessels heading towards Vancouver, and led outward-bound shipping towards First Narrows.

There was no keeper's house, but Captain W.D. Jones built himself a ramshackle shed from driftwood. The prospect of a royal visit by the Duke of York in 1901, however, led to a proper house being built, with the light set into the bedroom window.

Captain Jones, who served as keeper until he was 82, saved 16 lives, including eight from the tug *Chebalis*, which sank within seconds of being run down by the steamer *Princess Victoria* off Brockton Point in 1906. The present concrete edifice was designed and built in 1914 by Colonel William Anderson.

Cap des Rosiers Light

Gaspé, QC
Built: 1858
Style: Circular stone tower
No: H1768
Position: 48 51.4 N. 64 12.1 W
Focal plane: 134ft 6in (41m)
Range: 24 miles (39km)
Height: 88ft (27m)

The Cap des Rosiers Light stands at Land's End on the Gaspesie Peninsula along Highway 132 in Québec.

At 88ft, the stone-built lighthouse, with its boarded, circular red-roofed lantern, is the highest in Canada. Built in 1858, the tower was one of four lighthouses ordered by the Commissioners for Public Works, the others in the programme being the Anticosti West Point, Belle Isle and Point Amour Lights.

John Page, chief engineer, supervised their construction, while François Baby managed the work. Because Cap des Rosiers is so remote, the materials were delivered by sea, which was difficult during the winter months and slowed progress considerably. The tower was originally fitted with a first-order catadioptric lens powered by an Argand lamp that burned porpoise oil until coal oil became readily available in 1868.

Cape Bonavista Light

Bonavista Bay, NF
Built: 1843 and 1966
Style: Circular stone tower on dwelling
No: H0536
Position: 48 42.1 N. 53 05.2 W
Focal plane: 165ft (50m)

Range: 16 miles (26km)

The lighthouse is located on Cape Bonavista, Newfoundland. It was built between 1841 and 1843 to mark the entrances to Bonavista and Trinity Bays and to aid mariners headed for Labrador.

It was built on the northern tip of the peninsula that was probably the first land sighted by John Cabot, discoverer of North America, on the *Matthew* in 1497. In 1966 the light was moved to a framework tower nearby, and the original lighthouse was converted into a museum.

Cape d'Or Light

Minas Channel, NS
Built: 1875, 1922 and 1965
Style: Square concrete tower
No: H3938
Position: 47 17.5 N. 64 46.5 W
Focal plane: 79ft (24m)
Range: 13 miles (21km)

Cape d'Or is named for the golden hue of the incredible sunsets that can be witnessed in this location.

Cape d'Or was first marked with a fog whistle in 1875 to warn vessels of the hazardous rip tides in the Minas Channel.

The first lighthouse was erected on the banks of the Apple river in 1922 and was moved to the cape by boat, along with a new steam-powered fog signal.

The present concrete tower, built on the corner of a square white building, and with a red octagonal iron lantern, was built in 1965 and was automated in 1980.

The two keepers' dwellings are now used as an inn.

Cape Fourchu Light

Evangeline, NS
Built: 1839 and 1962
Style: Octagonal concrete tower
No: H3820
Position: 43 47.6 N. 66 09.3 W
Focal plane: 113ft 6in (34.5m)
Range: 13 miles (21km)

The first Cape Fourchu Light was an attractive octagonal wooden tower, built in 1839. The station is often the first sight ferry passengers, travelling from Bar Harbour and Portland, Maine, have as they enter Canada.

The much-photographed tower was replaced in 1962 with what locals were led to believe would be a replica, at least on the exterior. What they got, however, was a modern concrete edifice 77ft (23.5m) high, with red stripes tapered below the red polygonal metal lantern. This they disdainfully nicknamed 'the Apple Core'.

In 1980 Cape Fourchu became the monitoring station for other automated lighthouses in the area, but in 1993 the tower was itself automated, and the monitoring transferred to Letete, New Brunswick.

The new tower originally had a range of 22 miles (35km), but it was reduced to 13 miles in 1998, the same time that the foghorn was removed.

The site is now managed by the Friends of the Yarmouth Light Society, which has opened the 1912 keeper's house up to visitors.

Cape Scott Light

Vancouver Island, Queen Charlotte Sound,
BC
Built: 1927 and 1959
Style: Polygonal lantern on square structure
No: G5172
Position: 50 47.0 N. 128 25.5 W
Focal plane: 229ft (70m)
Range: 21 miles (34km)
Height: 29ft 6in (9m)

The Cape Scott Light was first established on
the north-west tip of Vancouver Island in
Queen Charlotte Sound in 1927.

The present stubby structure, built in
1959, shares the site with three keepers'
dwellings and an impressive-looking radio
mast.

Cape Spear Light

St. John's, Avalon, NF
Built: 1835 and 1955
Style: Octagonal pyramidal concrete tower
No: H0454
Position: 47 31.3 N. 52 37.3 W
Focal plane: 233ft (71m)

Range: 20 miles (32km)
Height: 35ft (10.5m)

Cape Spear is the most easterly point of North America. The first lighthouse was built here in 1835 to mark the approach to St. John's harbour and, though decommissioned in 1955, the 38-ft (11.5-m) circular stone tower, that rose from the centre of the square keeper's house, was Newfoundland's oldest standing light; the building is now a museum.

The present 35-ft concrete tower is fitted with a fourth-order dioptric lens and has a range of 20 miles.

227

Chantry Island Light

Port Elgin, Bruce Peninsula, Lake Huron,
ON
Built: 1859
Style: Conical stone tower with dwelling
Position: 44 29.2 N. 81 24.1 W
Focal plane: 103ft (31m)
Range: 6 miles (10km)
Height: 86ft (26m)

The 86-ft stone-built Chantry Island Light was designed to guide vessels towards Port Elgin.

Fitted with a second-order dioptric lens, the historic tower is one of six 'Imperial Lights', built by the British Imperial Lighthouse Service in 1859, on the Great Lakes. The others are at Christian Island, Cove Island, Griffith Island, Nottawasaga Island and Point Clark. The Chantry Island station was automated in 1954.

The tower is painted white with a bright red roof, lantern and trim. The lantern houses a second-order Fresnel lens.

The keeper's dwelling was only a shell of standing walls, having been destroyed by fire a number of years ago. In 1998, however, a local group met to form an organization to restore the keeper's quarters. By means of donations and other support, the Supporters of Chantry Island are well on their way to returning the station to its former glory.

Chantry Island was designated a Federal Migratory Bird Sanctuary in 1957 to protect the many birds nesting there.

Chebucto Head Light

Ketch Harbour, Halifax, NS
Built: 1872, 1940 and 1967
Style: Octagonal concrete tower
No: H3600
Position: 44 30.4 N. 63 31.4 W

Focal plane: 162ft (49m)
Range: 14 miles (22.5km)
Height: 45ft (14m)

A lighthouse at Chebucto Head was first established in 1872 to guide vessels towards

Ketch Harbour and Halifax, one of the finest natural harbours in the world. The lighthouse was replaced by a second tower in 1940, which is still standing. although it was superseded by the present 45-ft concrete tower in 1967.

Cove Island Light

Gig Point, Bruce Peninsula, Lake Huron,
ON
Built: 1858
Style: Conical limestone tower
Position: 45° 19.4 N. 81° 44.1 W
Focal plane: 101ft (31m)
Range: 16 miles (26km)
Height: 85ft (26m)

The Cove Island Light, located in Fathom Five National Marine Park, on the Bruce Peninsula, Ontario, has stood guard to warn Great Lakes mariners navigating the treacherous narrow channel between Lake Huron and Georgian Bay, since it became operational in October 1858.

While under construction, the crew kept a light burning on the island by placing a lantern at the top of the unfinished tower.

The Cove Island Light is similar in style to the other Imperial Lights on Chantry Island, at Point Clark and on Griffith Island.

The stone lightkeeper's cottage, lying adjacent to the tower, was built at the same time as the original lighthouse. A new lightkeeper's house was built in 1970 a short distance from the tower. The light station was continuously manned from 1858 to 1991, making it the longest keeper-occupied lighthouse in Ontario.

The lighthouse tower, the original house and fog plant, a workshop, the assistant keeper's house and the modern lightkeeper's house make up the light station as it stands today.

East Point Light

PE
Built: 1867
Style: Octagonal tower; red lantern and trim
No: H0920
Position: 46 27.1 N. 61 58.3 W
Focal plane: 100ft (30.5m)
Range: 20 miles (32km)
Height: 64ft (19.5m)

East Point is aptly named, being the easternmost point of land on Prince Edward Island and an ideal location for a lighthouse. It is one of the busiest aids to navigation in the province.

The East Point Light was built by William MacDonald in 1867 and, with its imposing white structure and red trimmings, remains a prime example of the standard Canadian octagonal design.

Initially, the lighthouse was positioned some distance inland and not, as Admiralty charts suggested, right on this easternmost point of Prince Edward Island. This confusion led to at least two shipwrecks, that of the Dominion line steamer *Québec* in 1879, and of the British HMS *Phoenix* in 1882. Three years after the latter drama, the lighthouse was moved to within 200ft (60m) of the point, only to be moved back again in 1908 when erosion threatened.

Fisgard Light

Victoria Harbour, Vancouver Island, BC
Built: 1860
Style: White conical tower, red lantern.
No: G5306
Position: 48 25.8 N. 123 26.8 W
Focal plane: 71ft (22m)
Height: 48ft (15m)

The Fisgard Lighthouse National Historic Site is in Colwood, British Columbia, on Fisgard Island at the mouth of Esquimalt Harbour.

Built in 1860, the lighthouse is the oldest in British Columbia, the 48-ft white conical granite tower having been designed and built by John Wright.

The station was automated in 1928, and the acetylene lamp in Fisgard's tower was replaced by a battery-powered electric light in the early 1940s. In 1950–51, a causeway was built out to Fisgard Island from the foreshore at Fort Rodd Hill by the Canadian Army; this was intended as a military obstacle, but also provided direct access to the Fisgard Light.

The former lighthouse keeper's residence is open to the public and contains displays and exhibits pertaining to the site's history. The attached tower is not open to the public, being an operational aid to navigation.

Five Islands Light

Sand Point, Minas Basin, NS
Built: 1914
Style: Square, pyramidal wooden tower
No: H4028
Position: 45 23.3 N. 64 04.1 W
Focal plane: 43ft (13m)
Range: 11 miles (18km)
Height: 33ft (10m)

The 33-ft Five Islands Light was built at Sand Point on the west side of the entrance to the East river in 1914 to guide vessels towards the Minas Basin, where the rise and fall of the tides are among the most extreme in the world. These fast-flowing waters cause considerable erosion and the lighthouse had to be moved in 1952, 1957 and finally in 1996, three years after it was decommissioned.

The Five Islands Lighthouse Preservation Society was formed in 1996, when Colchester County purchased the lighthouse and it was moved onto the property of Sand Point Campground. The society leases the lighthouse from the county and the land from Sand Point Campground for a nominal yearly sum. The new site is about 197ft (60m) from the previous location. The lighthouse is part of the Fundy Shore Ecotour.

Fort Amherst Light

St. John's Harbour, Avalon, NF
Built: 1813, 1852 and 1952
Style: Square, pyramidal wooden tower.
No: H0458
Position: 47 33.8 N. 52 40.8 W
Focal plane: 131ft 7in (40m)
Range: 13 miles (21m)
Height: 17ft (5m)

A lighthouse has stood on South Head, marking the entrance to St. John's harbour, since 1813. The original stone tower was built within the protected confines of Fort Amherst, and the garrison maintained the three whale-oil lamps with voluntary dues paid by those entering the harbour.

St. John's was one of the first European settlements in North America and the site was possibly visited, on St. John the Baptist's Day, 1497, by John Cabot in the *Matthew*.

By 1835, when responsibility for the light was transferred to the newly established Commissioners of Lighthouses, St. John's had become a thriving port. The light, however, was accurately described as 'quite a flimsy concern', and a second 39-ft (12-m) tower with an attached keeper's dwelling was built within the fort in 1852.

It was fitted with a fourth-order dioptric lens with a range of 16 miles (26km).

Part of the fort was demolished in 1952 to make way for the present 17-ft wooden tower.

Fort Point Light

Liverpool, NS
Built: 1855
Style: Square wooden tower on dwelling

Fort Point Light, the the fourth oldest in Nova Scotia, is in remarkably good shape for its age. It is situated at the southern entrance to Liverpool harbour.

As the transportation of lumber from this port became more important, and with the increased shipping that it entailed, the need for an additional light became apparent and the Fort Point Light was built in 1855.

The modest light was only 30ft (99m) high and was outfitted with three brass seal-oil lanterns with a range of only 8 miles (13km). Seal oil was later replaced with kerosene in 1864, but by 1951 the constant polishing of the reflectors had worn off the silver coating down to their copper bases. Electricity allowed the automation of the light and an upgrade to a sixth-order Fresnel lens, which was shut down in 1989.

The lighthouse had the lantern room on the top floor, while the ground floor held supplies and lamp oil. The second floor served as quarters for the keeper and his family but was so small that the first keeper moved to town and commuted to work. A kitchen was added in around 1900.

During World War II, weather forecasters were also assigned to the station, and in order to accommodate them, the keeper gave up his tower room and his family of five lived in the small kitchen. The keeper was paid an extra $36 per year to operate the hand-cranked fog horn from 1901 to 1951.

George's Island Light

Halifax Harbour, NS
Built: 1876, 1916 and 1919
Style: Octagonal concrete tower
No: H3618
Position: 44 38.4 N. 63 33.6 W
Focal plane: 59ft (18m)
Height: 54ft (16.5m)

George's Island is a glacial drumlin and the largest island entirely within the limits of Halifax harbour, located in Nova Scotia's Halifax Regional Municipality.

A lighthouse on George's Island – named after King George II of England – was first erected in 1876 to lead vessels into Halifax harbour.

The station has a unique history, for its original keeper, Robert Ross, served here from its first day until 1920, overseeing the building and operation of three successive lighthouses on the site.

The first wooden tower burned down in 1916 and a temporary light replaced it until the present 54-ft concrete tower was built in 1919. This tower, with a red stripe on the south side and a red aluminium lantern, was upgraded with a fourth-order dioptric lens in 1922, but a further 70 years passed before an electric lantern was installed. The station was automated in 1972 and is now the front light of the Halifax Harbour Inner Range.

Gibraltar Point Light

Toronto Harbour, Lake Ontario, ON
Built: 1808
Style: Octagonal brick tower
Position: 43 37.0 N. 79 22.6 W

Focal plane: 66ft (20m)
Range: 14 miles (22.5km)

The 62-ft (19-m) brown, brick-built Gibraltar Point Light, with its red polygonal lantern, standing on the south-western side of the point on Centre Island within Toronto Harbour, is the oldest standing lighthouse on the Great Lakes. The tower was decommissioned in 1959.

Louisbourg Light

Cape Breton East, NS
Built: 1734, 1842, 1924
Style: Octagonal pyramidal concrete tower
No: H3344
Position: 45 54.4 N. 59 57.5 W
Range: 21 miles (34km)
Height: 55ft (17m)

The original Louisbourg Light was built on Lighthouse Point, on the northern side of the harbour, by the French in 1734. It was the first in Canada and second in North America after the Boston Light (1716).

Louisbourg was built as a fortress port from which the French intended to hold New France against the English. The 68-ft (21-m) rubblestone tower, which was equipped with a circle of wicks burning cod-liver oil and set in a copper ring mounted on cork floats, was first lit on 1 April 1734. The heat from the flames was intense, and, on the night of 11 September 1736, the wooden supports within the lantern room caught fire. The tower survived and the light was temporarily replaced by a coal burner until a new 32-wick oil lamp was installed in 1738. The tower was destroyed by cannon fire during the British siege of Louisbourg in 1758 and was not replaced until 1842.

This second lighthouse was erected on the roof of a two-storey, wooden keeper's dwelling which was destroyed by fire in 1922. The present concrete lighthouse was completed in 1924 across the harbour from the old fortress, and is now automated.

Margaretsville Light

Bay of Fundy, NS
Built: 1859
Style: Square pyramidal tower
No: H3926
Position: 45 03.3 N. 65 04 W
Focal plane: 30ft (9m)
Range: 12 miles (19km)
Height: 21ft (6m)

The black-and-white 21-ft Margaretsville Light, with its broad black band and square white lantern, may be small in stature, but it figures prominently in the history of Canadian navigation lights.

Until the mid-1850s the Nova Scotia shoreline, around the Bay of Fundy, was largely unlit. The residents of Margaretsville decided that a lighthouse would attract more vessels to their harbour, and in 1859 Sir Brenton Haliburton agreed to allow the building of a public lighthouse on his land. Construction was supervised by William Earley, the first keeper, who had been steward to Sir Brenton. Earley was succeeded by his son John, who converted the second floor of the lighthouse into living quarters for use in bad weather. After John Earley's death, his widow, Ruth, continued the family profession and oversaw the replacement of the old lantern room with a cast-iron top in 1911.

The light was originally powered by eight red kerosene lamps with brass reflectors, which had to be cleaned each day and the reservoir refuelled with oil carried up from below until the tower was automated in 1963.

Medway Head Light

Port Medway, NS
Built: 1851, 1927, 1963 and 1983
Style: Square pyramidal wooden tower
No: H3722
Position: 44 06.2 N. 64 32.4 W

Focal plane: 79ft (24m)
Range: 13 miles (21km)
Height: 28ft 6in (9m)

The original Medway Head Light was a 23-ft (7-m) wooden tower built in 1851 to guide vessels towards Port Medway. The tower was rebuilt in 1927, then replaced with a conical fibreglass tower in 1963. The present 28ft 6-in concrete tower, with its square, white, red-roofed lantern, was erected in 1983 and was automated four years later.

Nootka Light

Vancouver Island, BC
Built: 1911 and 1968
Style: Square steel framework tower
No: G5219
Position: 49 35.6 N. 126 36.8 W

Focal plane: 101ft (31m)
Range: 17 miles (27km)
Height: 33ft (10m)

The first Nootka Light was a 37-ft (11-m) wooden tower erected in 1911 on the summit of San Rafael Island, close to Yuquot Point and Friendly Cove and facing Nootka Sound.

The present 33-ft tower was built in 1968. It has a square, white-painted enclosed stairwell in the centre and a red lantern.

North Cape Light

Northumberland Strait, PE
Built: 1865
Style: Octagonal wooden tower
No: H1076
Position: 47 03 N. 63 59 W
Focal plane: 78ft (24m)
Range: 18 miles (29km)

Height: 62ft (19m)

The 62-ft North Cape Light, with its red trim and red lantern, was built in 1865 on the north-western tip of Prince Edward Island to replace a portable lantern warning vessels away from what is the longest reef in North America.

The tower's original fourth-order dioptric light was replaced with a long-focus catoptric lens in 1875 and the station was finally electrified in 1975. Like other lighthouses on Prince Edward Island, the North Cape tower has had to be relocated to avoid the threat of eroding cliffs. The keeper's dwelling was pulled down in 1950.

Peggy's Point Light

St. Margaret's Bay, NS
Built: 1868, 1915
Style: Octagonal concrete tower
No: H3660
Position: 44 29.5 N. 63 55 W
Focal plane: 67ft (20.5m)

Range: 11 miles (18km)
Height: 50ft (15m)

The 50-ft concrete Peggy's Point Light, marking the eastern entrance to St. Margaret's Bay, is one of Canada's best-known icons. The present tower, known locally as Peggy's Cove Lighthouse, was built in 1915 to replace a wooden tower built above the keeper's dwelling that dated back to 1868. This had displayed a red light through a catoptric reflector, but the new tower had a white light, at first, which was changed to green in 1979.

Point Atkinson Light

Vancouver Harbour, BC
Built: 1875 and 1910
Style: Hexagonal concrete tower
No: G5426
Position: 49 19.8 N. 123 15.8 W
Focal plane: 108ft (33m)
Range: 20 miles (32km)
Height: 41ft (12.5m)

The original Point Atkinson Light, marking the entrance to English Bay and the Burrard Inlet, would have been lit in 1874 but for an administrative error in England, which led to the wrong light being shipped from Birmingham. As a result, the tower stood idle for a further winter until the correct optic could be obtained.

The present 41-ft concrete tower was built in 1910. In 1942, the station was armed with an 18-lb (8-kg) cannon, and Ken 'Gunfire' Brown, who served at the tower during World War II, gained some notoriety for firing warning shots at the slightest provocation. One shell, aimed across the bows of a fishing boat, skipped across the sound and went straight through the 9,600-ton freighter, *Fort Rae*, which had just been launched and was undergoing her first speed trials. Her captain was able to save his ship from sinking only by running her aground!

Point Clark Light

Eastern Shore, Lake Huron, ON
Built: 1859
Style: Conical stone tower
Position: 44 04.2 N. 81 45.3 W
Focal plane: 93ft (28m)
Range: 14 miles (22.5km)
Height: 90ft (27m)

Point Clark is one of six Imperial Lights constructed around Georgian Bay and the Bruce Peninsula by John Brown in the early to late 1850s. All six towers still stand, but the Point Clark Light is the only one of its kind to be located on the mainland, and is therefore accessible by vehicle.

The 90-ft high limestone tower warns mariners of a dangerous shoal which lies a few miles offshore. The tower is topped by a 12-sided lantern framed in cast iron.

The keeper's dwelling and garage also survive, the dwelling having been turned into a maritime museum owned by the Canadian Parks Service and operated by Huron Township.

The lighthouse has been proclaimed a Canadian National Historic Site, and continues to be an active aid to navigation.

Prim Point Light

Northumberland Strait, PE
Built: 1846
Style: Conical brick tower, red lantern
No: H0982
Position: 46 03 N. 63 02 W
Range: 20 miles (32km)

Height: 60ft (18m)

The 60-ft Prim Point Light, built by Richard Walsh in 1846 at the eastern entrance to Hillsborough Bay to guide vessels towards Charlottetown, is one of the few brick-built lighthouses in Canada.

The tower was designed by Isaac Smith, Prince Edward Island's most prominent 19th-century architect. It was originally named Hillsborough Bay Light and was equipped with a fourth-order Fresnel lens. The original keeper's dwelling was demolished when the tower was automated in 1969.

Puffin Island Light

Bonavista Bay, NF
Built: 1878
Style: Square pyramidal tower
No: H0556
Position: 49 03.7 N. 53 33.1 W
Focal plane: 70ft (21m)

Range: 14 miles (22.5km)
Height: 25ft (8m)

The first Puffin Island Light was a tower set on the end of a stone keeper's cottage built in 1878 to mark the entrance to Greenspond harbour.

The tower was fitted with a fourth-order dioptric lens and had a range of 12 miles (19km), although the beam was obscured by Big Pools Island in the north and Fox Island. The present 25-ft red-banded pyramidal tower provides a more powerful light with a range of 14 miles.

Rose Blanche Light

Rose Blanche Harbour, NF
Built: 1873 and 1940
Style: Granite building, light tower at one
 corner
No: H0244
Position: 47 36 N. 58 42.2 W
Focal plane: 50ft (15m)
Range: 8 miles (13km)

The original Rose Blanche Light was built in 1873 to mark the entrance to the harbour, and is known locally as the Cains Island Lighthouse.

It was transferred to a framework tower in 1940, and the old lighthouse became increasingly dilapidated. It has since been restored by a local historical group.

Sambro Island Light

Halifax Harbour, NS
Built: 1759
Style: Octagonal stone and concrete tower
No: H3632
Position: 44 26.2 N. 63 33.8 W
Focal plane: 140ft (43m)
Range: 24 miles (39km)
Height: 82ft (25m)

The Sambro Island Light is the oldest standing lighthouse in North America, and was the second light tower to be built in Canada.

The 82-ft stone tower, with its three red bands and red circular iron lantern, is sited at the centre of Sambro Island, 2 miles (3km) from the entrance to Halifax, one of the largest ice-free harbours in the world at this latitude.

It was built, at a time when Halifax was a major British naval port, to warn vessels of the 30 or more shoals at the entrance to the inlet. Initially the light, which was equipped with lamps burning fish oil, was neither efficient nor run with any kind of discipline.

The first keepers were government appointees who collected the harbour dues for themselves and neglected the lamps. Fish oil is notorious for its blackening smoke and the reflectors and glass were not always cleaned; moreover, much to the chagrin of crews attempting to reach Halifax harbour at night, the light was not always relit if the flame had gone out.

The loss of the Boston sloop, *Granby*, with all hands at the entrance to the harbour in 1771, brought matters to a head. A report on the tragedy accepted that '...the fatal accident happened for want of a light being properly kept in the lighthouse'. It also noted that naval ships had, on occasion, to fire at the lighthouse in order to make the keepers show a light. Glass flues were then installed over the lamps to carry off much of the smoke, but it was not until 1864 that a new lantern room

was installed. In 1906 the height of the tower was increased by 20ft (6m) and it was equipped with a first-order Fresnel lens.

Two years later the white-painted sentinel was given three red stripes to make it more easily visible in snow. In 1968, the lantern room was upgraded once more, this time with an aero-beacon, giving the light a range of 24 miles. The tower was automated in 1988 and has since undergone complete renovation, including extensive underpinning.

Seal Island Light

Seal Island, NS
Built: 1831
Style: Octagonal wooden tower
No: H3812
Position: 43 23.7 N. 66 00.8 W
Focal plane: 102ft (31m)
Range: 21 miles (34km)

Seal Island, 18 miles (29km) west of Cape Sable Island, lies off the south-west tip of Nova Scotia where the Bay of Fundy meets the Atlantic. Fog, storms and powerful tides have conspired to wreck more than 160 vessels on the three-mile-long island over the past three centuries, making it one of the most notorious maritime graveyards on the Atlantic coast. Those who managed to make it ashore, on this remote and barren island, invariably died from exposure during the winter months, and ministers made a pilgrimage to the island during the first weeks of spring to bury their remains.

The 68-ft (21-m) Seal Island Light was built in 1831 as part of a sea-rescue base set up to reduce the number of maritime disasters, while a steam-powered fog whistle was established nearby in 1870, replaced by a diaphone in about 1900. The original light was powered by seal oil until replaced by a kerosene lamp in 1892. A second-order revolving Fresnel lens was installed in 1902, and the station was finally electrified in 1959. In 1978 the Fresnel lens was replaced with an aero-marine beacon and the station became semi-automatic.

In 1986 the keepers' families were moved off the island and the station changed to rotational status, with teams of two keepers working alternate 28-day shifts. The light was automated in 1990 and is now monitored by the lightkeepers at the Machias Seal Island East Light.

Swallowtail Light

Grand Manan Island, NB
Built: 1860
Style: Octagonal tower with a red lantern.
Focal Plane: 122ft (37m)
Range: 12 nautical miles
Height: 53ft (16m)

From its rocky outcrop on Grand Manan Island, in New Brunswick, the Swallowtail Light stands watch and has adorned this peninsula since 1860. The lighthouse is situated on a piece of land that is almost detached from the rest of the island and can be reached only by a footbridge.

The buildings once housed the two lighthouse keepers and their families, but have since been turned into a bed and breakfast establishment. This is a beautiful place on which to rest for a day or two and enjoy the beauty of Grand Manan Island. The lighthouse is still in operation.

Western Head Light

Liverpool, NS
Built: 1962
Style: Octagonal tower with red lantern
Focal plane: 55ft (17km)
Range: 14 nautical miles

The Western Head Light is situated on the western side of the entrance to Liverpool Bay in Nova Scotia.

The site was originally a fog alarm station in 1930 and expanded to include the Western Head Light in 1962. Today, the facility serves as an Environment Canada Weather Station. The light was destaffed in 1988 but will play a role for mariners in the future as part of navigation by GPS (Global Positioning System).

Wood Islands Main Light

Northumberland Strait, PE
Built: 1876
Style: Square pyramidal wooden tower
No: H0962
Position: 45 57 N. 62 44 W
Focal plane: 71ft 6in (22m)
Range: 12 miles (19km)
Height: 52ft 6in (16m)

The Wood Islands Main Light, which rises from a red-roofed dwelling and has a red lantern, was built in 1876 to guide the ferries crossing Northumberland Strait to Pictou, Nova Scotia. This 'pepper-pot'-style tower was equipped with a fourth-order Fresnel lens and a range of 15 miles (24km), downgraded when the lighthouse was electrified in 1958 to 12 miles. The station was automated in 1991.

Wood Islands Range Lights

Northumberland Strait, PE
Built: 1902
Style: Front Range: white square tower and lantern, rising from a small white building with sloping walls, red trim
No: H0964 (Front Light)
Focal plane: 24ft (7m)
Range: 6 miles (10km)
Height: 19ft (6m)
No: H0964.1 (Rear Light)
Style: White, square, pyramidal wooden tower with red stripe and white square lantern
Focal plane: 37ft (11m)
Range: 7 miles (11km)
Height: 32ft (10m)

The pair of lighthouses that make up Wood Islands Range Lights were built in 1902 on the east training pier to guide vessels into Wood Islands harbour. Originally, both range lights were red and visible over a 6-mile range. When they were moved in 1940, their beams were changed to white, then in 1963 to green; they assumed their present flashing mode in 1967.

INDEX

ACKNLOWEDGEMENTS

Front Cover: © Lori Lebraque/Shutterstock. Back Cover: ©Jeff Schultes/Shutterstock. The following interior images were supplied through Shutterstock © courtesy of the following photographers: Andy Z: page 183. Anthony Ricci: page 79. Bill Florence: page 25 right. Carlos E Santa Maria: page 97. Colin D. Young: page 63. Comosaydice: page 23. Dave Wetzel: page 196. David Gaylor: page 189. Doug Lemke: pages 8-9, 36, 69. Elena Fernandez Zabelgue/skaya: page 160.Elena Terletskaya: Page 10 left. Eugene Moerman: page 103. Frank Jr.: page 20.Freddy Eliasson: page 174. Ggw1962: page 227. Greg Kushmerek: page 16.Henry E Stamm: page 27 right. Henryk Sadura: page 105. How I see life: page 232.Iofoto: page 129. Jeffry M Frank: page 21. Jeff Bankel:page 195. Jeff Schultes: pages 37 right, 71. John Brueske: page 125. John Sartin: page 187. Kamira: page 11. Karhmanduphotog: page 192. Kenneth Keifer: page 31. LL Masseth: page 201. Loraine Kouratas: page 82. Lori Lebraque: page 45. Lotzov: page 245. Mary Terriberry: pages 15, 91, 128. Michael Hynes: page 17. Mike Clime: page 244. Moutain Pix: page 14 below. Natalia Brataslvsky: page 190. Nelson Sirlin: page 25 left. Norman Pogson: page 223. Paul Murtagh: page 12. Pecold: page 13. Peter Kunasz: page 178. PHB.C2 (Richard Smik): pages 70, 152. Plearn: page 90. Robert Paul Vanbeets: page 10 right. S. Borisov: page 6-7. SNEHIT: page 99. South Bay Lee: page 200. Stephanie Bidouze: page 14 above. Steve Haeap: page 26. Stuart Monk: page 30. Susan Montgomory: page 102. Sylvana Rega: page 55. Terrence Mendoza: page 89. Terry Reimini: page 107. Terry Straehley: page 176. TFoxFoto: page 185. Thomas Barrat: page 151. Tim Yuan: page 242. The following photographs were supplied through Flickr/Creative Commonswww.creativecommons.org /Wikimedia Commons/GNU licences by the following photographers: Abarndweller: pages 3, 115. Abmaac: page 146. A.M. Kuchling: page 165. Andrea Schaffer: page 221. Anita Ritenour: page 186. Anne632: pages 101 both, 104, 110, 112, 179. Anne Hornyak: page 124. Anthony Rabun: page 133. April Lionsatthegate: page 54. Artico2: page 211. ©©Arthur D. Chapman and Audrey Bendus: page 184. Arturodonate: page 167. Ashtray: page: 64. Aude: page 78 right. Beige Alert: page 111. Billau: page 123. Binnurgul: page 191. Bob Jagendorf: page 243. Bpeninsula: page 230. Brian.gratwicke: page 168. Canadian Coastguard: page 257. Cdamgen: page: 150. Chriswsn: page 149. Cliff1066: 41. Cwbash: page 116. CWWYCOFF1: pages 94, 108. Dana Moos Realtor: page 77. Dave Sizer: page 188. David Baron: page 193 Dennis Jarvis: pages, 2, 18 left, 218, 224, 225, 229, 233, 235, 236, 238, 240, 249, 250. Doug Kerr: page 83. Ebyabe: pages 126, 135, 157, 163, 169. Ed Bierman: page 205. Eldar Kamalov: page 87. EndMstr: page 216. Erik Hansen: page 62. Explore the Bruce: page 228. Fletcher6: page 61. Galwia Dreyzina: page 33. G. McFly: page 156. Greg Kushmerek: page 29. Headharbourlight: page 28. Heliotrop3: page 220. Henryk Sadura: page 32. Hoki69: page 35. James L Woodward: page 48 right. Jan Kranendonk: page 24. Jason Sturner72: page 98. Jef Poskanzer: page 198. Jens Alpers: page 53. Jkirkhart35: pages 194, 210. Joanna Poe: page 234. J O'Brien: page 219. Joe Mabel: page 206. Johncab: page 138. John Phelan: page 59 Jordan Kalilich: page 148. Jsfouche: page 74. JulieJules: page 81. Kadin2048: page 88. Kathleen Tyler Conkin: page 96. Kennstilger47: page 217. Kevin Marsh: page 109. Kretyn: page 114. L'eau Bleue: page 67. Leonard J DeFrancisci: page 132. Linda Tanner: page 177. Littlelioncat: page 47. Liza Phoenix: page 175. Magnolia1000: page 248. Malo: page 137. Martin Cathrae: pages 231, 246. Mary Terriberry: page 50. Matt Dempsey: page 95. MattK1979: page 145. Matt Schilder: page 147. Mike Reichold: page 143. Mingo.nl: page 153. Ming-Yen HSU: page 208. Mr T in DC: pages 22, 139, 141, 164. NASA: page 131. NOAA Photo Library: pages 92, 155 both, 199. Nsandel: page 181. Paparlars: page 209. Paul Markham: page 117. Petersbar: page 49. Paul Hamilton: page 253. Polaron: page 85. Puroticorico: page 118. Pwrockett: page 134. Randy Pertiet: page 171. Rapidfire: page 57. RDECOM: page 159. Rkramer62: page 136. Rona Proudfoot: page 106. Runneralan 2004: page 42. Rushangm: page 207. Sailn1: page 161. Sanfranman59: page 197. Sarah and Jason: page 78 right. Scott Catron: page 182. Scott D. Sullivan: page 214. Scott Ray: page 76. Selflearner1: page 237. Sharedferret: page 251. Sharpteam: page 34. Shipwrecklog: page 113, 121, 122. Shoothead: page 86. Shortlake's Hobby: page 239. Stan Kruslicky: page 158. Stefan Hillebrand: pages 43, 75. Steven Frame: page 172. Su-Laine: page 226. Susan Simon: page 65. Suzanne Tucker: page 120. Swampyank: page 68. Tbeach: page 44. Ted Kerwin: pages 46, 48 left, 58, 60, 66, 72, 154. This is Bossy: page 80. Thomas: page 201. Tim Gage: page 241. T Maggio: pages 4, 52. TriggBb(isaway): page 93. TWP: page 40. US Coastguard: pages 118, 119, 127, 142, 166, 173, 213. US Federal Government: page 162. US Fish and Wildlife Service: page 73, 170. US Navy: page 202. VJ Matthews: page 222. Warfieldian: page 140. Woodlot: page 130. www.birdsphotos.com: page 144. Zensrokoner: page 201. Zhong54: page 189. Library of Congress: page 18 right. Wikimedia Commons: page 19 all, 39.